The Mother of Necton

This book is dedicated to my
grandmother, Eliza Ong;
to my mother, who encouraged
me to write it; and to the Ong,
Brown and Crockley descendants
wherever they are.

The Mother of Necton

A Century of Norfolk Life

Mary Nichols

breedon **books**
PUBLISHING

First published in Great Britain in 2000 by
The Breedon Books Publishing Company Limited
Breedon House, 3 The Parker Centre, Derby, DE21 4SZ.

ISBN 1 85983 217 2

Printed and bound by Butler & Tanner Ltd., Selwood
Printing Works, Caxton Road, Frome, Somerset.

Colour separations and jacket printing by
GreenShires Group Ltd., Leicester.

Contents

Acknowledgements

This book could not have been written without the help of a great many people and I would like to thank them here: My brother, John VanderVlies and my cousins, Philip Ong, Joan Long and Angela Pickering, for their memories, personal stories, and pictures.

Mrs Edna Smale, Eliza's niece in Canada and Mrs Joyce Robinson for information about Alice. Mrs Dolly Bell, Mrs Hilda Saunders, Mrs Enid Makins, Mrs Brenda Firman, Mrs Pauline Tennant, Mrs Freda Bowcock, Mrs Colleen Wilkin, Mr Colin Howlett, Mr Brian Hubbard, Mrs Kathy Parker, Mrs Gladys Hart and Mr and Mrs David Willis for photographs and much information.

Mrs Honor Yaxley for information about the Baptist chapel; Rev. Peter Taylor and Mrs Joan Borgars of Necton church; Mrs Freda England, Heacham church warden; Rev. John Smith, Vicar of Swaffham; The Rector of Holt.

Also the Norfolk Records office; Swaffham Museum; the Royal College of Midwives; the United Kingdom Central Council for Nursing, Midwifery and Health Visiting; Mr David Tyrell, the Archivist to Middlesbrough Borough Council and Mr Terry Gilder of the *North East Evening Gazette* for information about Charles Ong's death; The *Eastern Daily Press*; the Imperial War Museum; the archivist of the Guards Museum and Sir Samuel Roberts Bart. of Cockley Cley Hall.

Special thanks to my cousin Dulcie Kenning for helping me track down contacts in Necton, to Kate Wyer-Roberts for the map of Necton, and last but by no means least, my sister, Ann Barnes, to whom I owe a special thanks for spending so many hours searching the records at the Norwich Records Office on my behalf.

Introduction

MY GRANDMOTHER, Eliza Ong, was a countrywoman, small and neat and completely unflappable with an indomitable courage and a prodigious capacity for hard work. Because she was always willing, cheerful and discreet, she became the village nurse and midwife, the person everyone turned to in times of need, 'the woman you sent for' in the parlance of the times. From World War I until the advent of the National Health Service in 1948, when she was well into her sixties, she helped new people into the world and eased the going from it of those who were dying, and she saved many a life by her skill and devotion.

Eliza would never reveal her age; she became impervious to hints and when anyone resorted to a direct question, would answer with a twinkle in her eye and a stubbornness that was characteristic of her, 'As old as my tongue and a little older than my teeth.' As she approached her century, relatives with an eye to a telegram from the Queen, made strenuous efforts to discover the truth, but she insisted she did not want to live to be 100. She got her wish and kept us guessing to the very end.

In uncovering the reason for this I found myself transported back in time, living her early life with her, experiencing the sorrows and the joys, and her love of her family, which extended to everyone around her. It was not a cloying love, not particularly demonstrative, but it was there, solid and dependable as she was. This is the story of her life and the small country community in which she lived, told through the eyes of her grandchildren and others who knew and loved her, and through her own vividly recounted tales that evoked so faithfully the times in which she lived.

THE FAMILY TREE

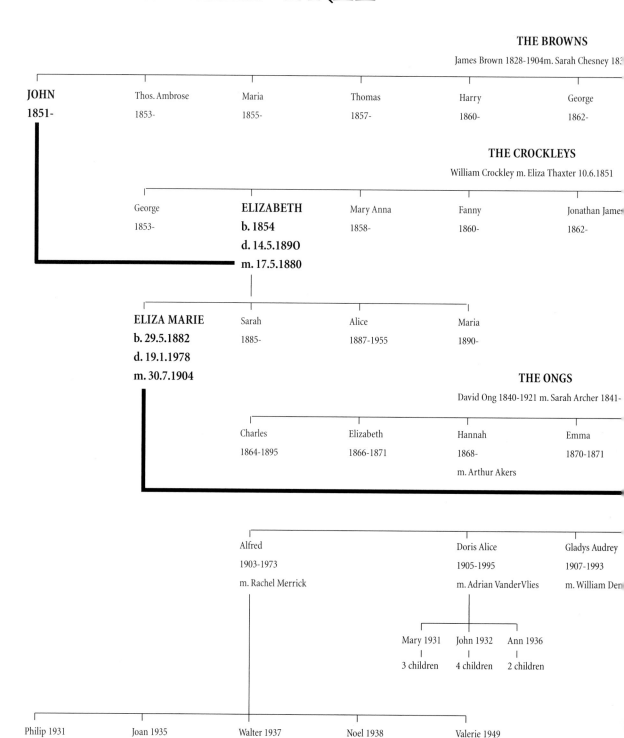

THE BROWNS

James Brown 1828-1904 m. Sarah Chesney 183

JOHN	Thos. Ambrose	Maria	Thomas	Harry	George
1851-	1853-	1855-	1857-	1860-	1862-

THE CROCKLEYS

William Crockley m. Eliza Thaxter 10.6.1851

George	**ELIZABETH**	Mary Anna	Fanny	Jonathan James
1853-	**b. 1854**	1858-	1860-	1862-
	d. 14.5.1890			
	m. 17.5.1880			

ELIZA MARIE	Sarah	Alice	Maria
b. 29.5.1882	1885-	1887-1955	1890-
d. 19.1.1978			
m. 30.7.1904			

THE ONGS

David Ong 1840-1921 m. Sarah Archer 1841-

Charles	Elizabeth	Hannah	Emma
1864-1895	1866-1871	1868-	1870-1871
		m. Arthur Akers	

Alfred	Doris Alice	Gladys Audrey
1903-1973	1905-1995	1907-1993
m. Rachel Merrick	m. Adrian VanderVlies	m. William Den

Mary 1931	John 1932	Ann 1936
3 children	4 children	2 children

Philip 1931	Joan 1935	Walter 1937	Noel 1938	Valerie 1949
5 children	5 children	3 children	I child	3 children

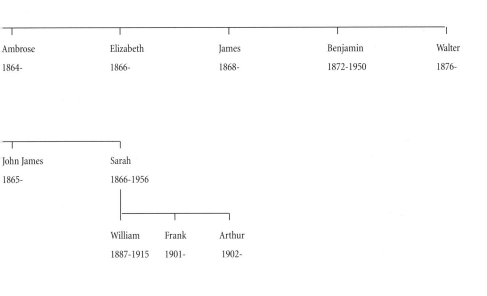

Ambrose	Elizabeth	James	Benjamin	Walter
1864-	1866-	1868-	1872-1950	1876-

John James	Sarah
1865-	1866-1956

William	Frank	Arthur
1887-1915	1901-	1902-

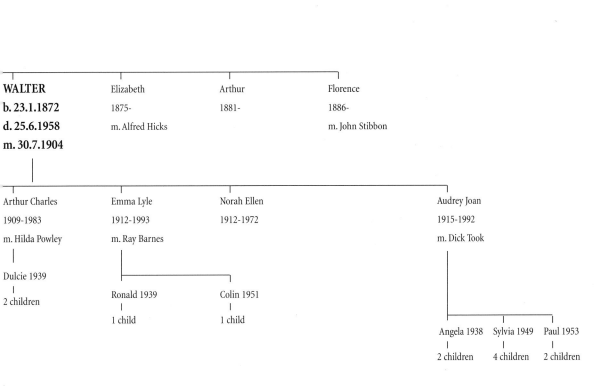

WALTER	Elizabeth	Arthur	Florence
b. 23.1.1872	1875-	1881-	1886-
d. 25.6.1958	m. Alfred Hicks		m. John Stibbon
m. 30.7.1904			

Arthur Charles	Emma Lyle	Norah Ellen	Audrey Joan
1909-1983	1912-1993	1912-1972	1915-1992
m. Hilda Powley	m. Ray Barnes		m. Dick Took

Dulcie 1939
2 children

Ronald 1939	Colin 1951
1 child	1 child

Angela 1938	Sylvia 1949	Paul 1953
2 children	4 children	2 children

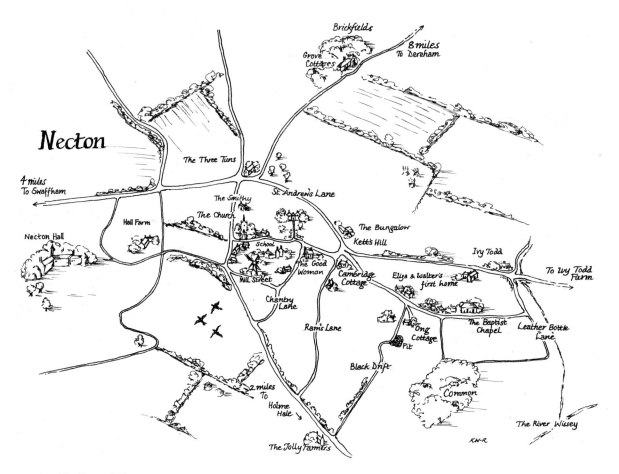

Necton

Brickfields

Grove
Cottages

8 miles
To Dereham

4 miles
To Swaffham

The Three Tuns

St. Andrew's Lane

The Smithy

The Church

The Bungalow

Hall Farm

Kett's Hill

Necton Hall

Ivy Todd

School

The Good
Woman

To Ivy Todd
Farm

Mill Street

Cambridge
Cottage

Eliza & Walter's
first home

Chantry
Lane

The Baptist
Chapel

Leather Bottle
Lane

Ram's Lane

Ong
Cottage

Pit

Black Drift

Common

2 miles
To
Holme Hale

The River Wissey

K·N·R

The Jolly Farmers

The old village of Necton.

Sunny Days in Necton

AS A FAMILY we moved about quite a lot when I was a child, usually in towns and suburbs, so being taken to stay with Grandma Ong for the holidays was pure heaven. My mother would stay for a day or two and then go back alone, leaving me, my brother and my sister with our grandparents. Often there were cousins there too.

My grandparents owned a smallholding in Necton, which was, and is, a farming village in Norfolk. It is four miles

View of Black Drift from the pit. The cottage is on the right.

Mary, John and Ann at the cottage door.

from Swaffham, the nearest town. Motor cars were so infrequent along its narrow byways that it never occurred to our grandparents to restrain us or warn us to watch the traffic and 'look both ways', a dogma hammered into us by constant repetition at home. We were free to wander along leafy lanes, across meadows and commons, to paddle in ditches, chase butterflies or gather blackberries until hunger drove us back to the cottage at the top end of Black Drift where our grandparents and our unmarried Aunt Norah lived.

The Drift had been surfaced for only a couple of hundred yards, from the road at the top as far as my grandparents' home and the small cottage that stood opposite. From there it petered into a grassy, deeply-rutted track that wound its way between hedges and ditches for a mile or so to another road, this time a proper tarmac one, that joined Necton to Holme Hale. It was just passable with a car, if you were not too concerned for its springs, but apart from my grandfather's pony and trap I never saw traffic bigger than a bicycle or tractor on it.

There was a meadow down the Drift where rabbits played, and if we sat down quietly and kept very still we could watch them a long time before they caught our scent and scampered off. There were mushrooms too, and wild flowers in plenty; daisies for making chains and buttercups for holding under your chin where the yellow reflection on your skin was supposed to tell if you liked butter. In due season there were cowslips, known as paigles, primroses, yarrow, campion and honeysuckle, colts-foot, harebells, foxgloves and poppies, called 'headache' by my grandmother. I never failed to take a bunch of these flowers home to Grandma. They were received gladly, arranged in a jam jar on a window sill and not thrown out until they were all well and truly dead.

Along the hedge by the ditch enormous dragonflies zoomed, their iridescent bodies and transparent wings bright against the dark foliage. My grandfather called them 'hoss-stingers', which I thought was an ugly name for so beautiful a creature. There were butterflies too: meadow browns, painted ladies, peacocks, red admirals and cabbage whites, which Aunt Norah hated because their caterpillars ate the cabbages. Before long we knew the names of them all, and learned the strange names our grandparents had for other creatures: lady-birds were bushy barnabees, ants were bishimeers, and snails were hodmadods. Goldfinches were draw-waters and wood pigeons ringdaws; a thrush was a mavis, a chaffinch a spink.

In autumn we filled our pockets with horse chestnuts and hazelnuts and some-times we ventured out of the end of the Drift and crossed the Holme Hale road to a meadow where the biggest and juiciest blackberries grew. If we had remembered to bring a receptacle and a hook, we gathered some and carried them triumphantly back to see them made into jelly or put into pies with windfall apples from the orchard.

The village seemed never to have taken the plunge into the 20th century. The pace of life was slow, the Squire was still the Squire, and children were still expected to mind their manners. The old village crafts-men – the miller, the wheelwright, the blacksmith, the saddler and harness maker, the butcher, the shoemaker, and the dress-maker were still in evidence, though disap-pearing fast. By the time World War II ended, they would be gone forever. The dim little shops in the front rooms of some of the cottages, which sold groceries, patent medicines, brushes and brooms, hardware, twine, rope, nails, lamp wicks, paraffin, sta-tionery, and accumulator batteries for the wireless, were also destined to disappear or become self-service mini-markets.

My grandparents were true Victorians and their lives must have followed almost the same daily pattern as they had at the turn of the century over thirty years before, which does not mean they were narrow-minded or incapable of enjoyment. Grandma, in particular, had a keen sense of humour. They lived by the maxim, 'Early to bed, early to rise, makes a man healthy, wealthy and wise.' I am not sure about the wealth, for they never had very much of that, unless you count love, respect, and contentment, which they had in abundance.

Their cottage in Black Drift had no elec-tricity, sewer or mains drains; water was drawn as needed from one of the deepest wells in the county. The water sometimes contained wriggling things in it, but Grandad maintained they were harmless and were a sign of its purity. Wriggling things aside, I know it tasted better than anything that came out of a tap at home. You had to let the bucket down gently so that it barely skimmed the surface before tipping it slightly to fill it. If you let it down with a clatter it upended and would not fill properly and you risked the bucket falling off its chain, and then it was lost.

The garden was given over almost entirely to fruit and vegetables. Gooseberries, blackcurrants and redcurrants grew around the privy. A large rhubarb patch covered the ground beside the garden wall, and in the middle bed there were rows of potatoes, runner beans and peas, onions, cabbages and carrots. My grandfather would pull a carrot, knock the earth off it and hand it to me to eat. If I complained that it was dirty, I was told, 'Tha' oon't hurt you. You hatta eat a peck o' dirt afore you die,' and I would wipe the carrot on my apron and eat it contentedly.

A few flowers were allowed to grow each side of the path to the door. In spring daffodils, called daffy-down-dillies, and wallflowers whose other name of gilly flowers I liked better, filled the air with their scent, and later on, marigolds, lupins and delphiniums, lilies and heavily scented stocks, were followed by asters and Michaelmas daisies, old-fashioned country flowers that could be relied upon to grow year after year and did not take a lot of looking after.

Besides the garden there was an orchard, which was really only a meadow in which stood several very old and very gnarled fruit trees. One of these grew almost horizontally and was always referred to as the 'lay-down' tree. It was ideal for climbing and I would while away many an hour in its topmost branches. There was a rope swing attached to another of the trees and one year, when a large tree was felled nearby, my grandfather made a seesaw with a plank across a section of its trunk. He called it a 'titty-ma-tawty'. In the corner of the orchard there was a pigsty, a cart shed where the trap was kept, and a couple of

hen houses, though the hens spent more time out of them than in and we had to search the hedgerows every day for their hidden eggs; truly free range. A meadow next to the orchard housed half a dozen calves or sheep and beyond that was a field given over each year to crops.

Eliza feeding the ducks watched by her daughter, Norah, mid-1920s. The right-hand side of the building behind her was used as a pigsty. The left side of the building was where the trap was kept.

On the far side of the orchard was 'the pit', a huge, very deep, very murky pond into which the villagers habitually tipped their rubbish, much to Grandad's annoyance. It had a fatal fascination for the locals; in summer they tried swimming in it and in winter skating on it, with dire results. By the 1930s, my grandfather had already pulled 17 near-drowned bodies from it, one of whom was his own three-year-old daughter and another a village child who was later to become his daughter-in-law, Hilda Powley.

Hilda was 13 at the time and, according to her father, old enough to know better. But she went in trying to rescue her 10-year-old brother and 8-year-old sister, who had been tempted to see if the ice would bear. Luckily my grandfather was ploughing in a nearby field and ran when he heard their screams. Guessing the cause, he took the reins from the horse with him and used them to haul the children out. It was so cold their clothes were freezing on them, but fortunately it was a Monday and my grandmother had the copper on the boil. They were taken up to the house and put, fully clothed, into warm baths, given hot sweet tea and, when they were warm enough, sent home in an assortment of garments belonging to my aunts and uncles.

My mother was the culprit when her sister went into the pit. Her older brother had seen a big fish and called her to have a look at it. Without thinking she let go of the handles of the pushchair in which Emma was strapped. In no time it had rolled down the steep slope and turned upside down in the water. This time my grandfather, dashing down the Drift to the rescue, was helped by the Squire's gamekeeper who was cycling by at the time. More hot baths and strong sweet tea.

There were other incidents, including a party of young men and women from the Hall who arrived by motor car and pro-ceeded to strap on skates before venturing on to the ice. As ever, Grandad was not far away. Toffs or not, he gave them a piece of his mind before sending them home. The pit was the only place we children were strictly forbidden to go.

The cottage in which my grandparents lived was built of brick and flint, and was typical of the area. It had once, many years before, been two labourers' dwellings, each containing one room at ground level and another above it, reached by a tortuous half-circular stairway beside a chimney breast. Next to the cottage and end on to the road were the 'wash'us' and the 'middle shud'. The wash-house fire was lit at dawn every Monday, and clouds of steam would issue from the copper hanging above it for the rest of the day. Beside the copper stood an old table and an array of baths in different shapes and sizes, which were used for rinsing the clothes. There was always a blue bag in the rinsing water to make the whites white. The shed next door housed the family bicycles and a big iron mangle, the handle of which I sometimes helped to turn for want of something better to do. When the sparkling white washing was flapping in the breeze of the orchard, my grandmother would go across the road to her neighbour and tell her the copper was full of boiling soapy water and that she was welcome to use it, if she had washing to do.

On the other side of the middle shed was a wooden stable, always referred to as the 'end shud', which in those early days was the home of the pony that pulled the trap. A harness and bits of tackle hung on the post at the end of the pony's stall. The walls were hung with old farm implements, scythes, sickles, flails, weed hooks and any number of mysterious iron objects, as well as leather tackle and storm lanterns. There were blackened oak bins for cattle and chicken feed, trays for storing apples and racks for hay and straw. It was dark and warm and smelled deliciously musty and countrified.

In the house itself, the stairs had been pulled out of the kitchen end and the space shelved to make a cupboard for saucepans and cooking utensils; another cupboard on the other side of the fireplace was used as a larder, and a third contained crockery and glasses. A big table, covered in patterned oilcloth, stood against the wall opposite the kitchen range. Behind the door stood Grandad's Windsor chair, which no one else dare occupy, and beside that a small table on which stood a couple of primus stoves. These were used for cooking vegetables and boiling water when the heat of summer made lighting the fire in the black range unbearable, except on baking days when there was no help for it and we cooked along with the cakes.

The second downstairs room was used when special visitors arrived and for Sunday tea and Christmas. Sometimes I used to sit at the dining table in there to write dutifully to my parents, crayon picture books or look at my grandmother's scrapbooks. These contained a kaleidoscope of postcards, Christmas and birthday cards, snapshots, newspaper cuttings, notices, even scraps of cloth, anything she had thought worth preserving, and they fascinated me because she nearly always had a story to tell with each one.

The steep, bending stairs beside the fireplace in the sitting room led directly into the room above, so that if we were making too much noise after we went to bed and Grandad was obliged to come after us, it was his disembodied head that appeared first at floor level. 'Howd yar nize t'gither!' he would say. He rarely had to come up any further before we subsided into silence.

The first bedroom had lino and homemade rag rugs on the floor, which had a very definite slope towards the second bedroom. It contained a double iron bedstead with brass rails and a knob on each corner, which young fingers soon discovered could be unscrewed and detached. On the bed was a thick feather mattress. There was the usual washstand in the room, on which stood a matching bowl, jug, and soap dish. The jug stood in the bowl and was filled every day with fresh water. Also on the washstand stood a clear glass carafe of drinking water with a tumbler upended over it. Inside the washstand cupboard were a couple of matching chamber pots, which went under the bed after use. The second bedroom was almost identical to the first, except that it held two single beds instead of a double and its floor sloped even more crazily towards the corner, where the stairs from the kitchen had once emerged in the days when it was a separate cottage.

Nothing was straight. I remember when my grandmother and aunt decided to wallpaper the sitting room, Grandma grumbled that the walls were all 'slanterdicular' and they 'dussn't' use a patterned paper because they would never be able to match it.

There was no indoor lavatory of course. The privy was a small hut down the garden path. It contained a wooden seat with a bucket underneath, which was emptied regularly and stealthily by Grandad. But the smallest room, with its carefully cut up squares of newspaper hanging on a hook, was surprisingly not an unpleasant place to be.

This tiny cottage was certainly inadequate in terms of sleeping arrangements, which was why 'the hut' had been built. This was a sturdy wooden building standing sideways on from the cottage and was separated from the kitchen wall by a sort of open-sided scullery. This scullery was always referred to as 'the back place', though it was not at the back of the house at all. The real back of the cottage abutted a small pasture and had no door, although it did have two very tiny windows, one up and one down. The light coming through the downstairs window was often blocked by the inquisitive animals that grazed in the field.

The back place was used for all kitchen jobs except cooking. The washing up was done out there, chickens plucked, vegetables prepared, and shoes polished. It was where Grandad shaved with a cut-throat razor, stropping it on a leather that hung near a pitted mirror on a cupboard in the corner. And here we performed our early morning ablutions.

'The water's cold,' I would complain, to which my hardy and weather-beaten grandfather would say, 'Hot water meks you soft. Come on, git on with it and git yar vittels.' And when he was not looking my grandmother, with a twinkle in her eye and a finger on her lips, would tip the big blackened kettle up over the bowl so that the water was at least tepid.

I never saw any of the adults in the family take a bath, which is not to say they did not; I suppose such personal niceties were left until children were safely in bed. But on Mondays, when the copper was lit and plenty of hot water was available, it was brought by the jug-full from the wash house to the kitchen hearth where the long galvanised bath had been taken from its hook on the back place wall to receive it. I liked to have my bath when my grandfather was busy elsewhere, because if he took a hand in the proceedings I was literally scrubbed all over and emerged pink and thoroughly resentful.

Grandad was not a big man, but he had a 'presence' and an unwavering belief in the rightness of doing things his way. He had light, gingery hair – to me it did not seem particularly grey – and a bristly chin that he shaved as often as he saw fit. He wore brown serge trousers held up with a broad leather belt, and a collarless striped shirt that he dressed up on occasion with a white neckerchief. The only time I saw him wearing a collar and tie was at the weddings of his children. Out of doors he plodded about in rubber ankle boots with laces; indoors he changed into felt slippers. His word was law and disobedience was not to be tolerated. I was a little afraid of him and always assumed everyone else was too, from my grandmother downwards.

I remember once complaining bitterly to my mother that Grandad had taken his belt off to me, hoping she would take my side in my grievance with my grandfather (a grievance so slight I cannot even remember what it was now). I had probably 'answered back', a failing of mine and a particularly heinous crime in my grandfather's eyes.

'What did you do?' my mother asked. I think she meant what had I done to deserve his wrath, but I misunderstood her. 'I ran away,' I said.

Grandchildren, Philip and Mary, 1938.

as we were told without being smacked. There's no reason to suppose he's changed.'

'But he took his belt off.'

'He always did that.' My mother smiled as if remembering something that had happened long ago. 'It was a threat and it was enough; he never needed to do anything else.'

I remember being amazed at this revelation, being convinced that Grandad had ruled his family with the aid of that belt with its big brass buckle.

My brother told me he was never sure whether to be more worried about the beating he was about to receive or whether Grandad's trousers would fall down. He would lift the belt just as Grandma came out of the house behind him. 'Pa,' she would say without raising her voice, 'let the boy be.' Grandad would grunt his annoyance, replace his belt round his middle, and stomp off down the garden path. Her timing was impeccable. On one occasion Grandma was not around. Grandad, with his arm poised to strike, waited in vain for her admonishment. So did John, with his heart in his mouth. After a moment of frustrated impatience, Grandad put his belt on again and went off, grumbling. Our cousin, Philip, told me he received the same treatment, usually because he had disobeyed orders and been down to the pit to fish for tiddlers.

My grandmother I adored, and so did everyone else. She was always hurrying off at a moment's notice, leaving Aunt Norah in charge of whatever she happened to be doing at the time. Sometimes she would be gone all night and arrive home at breakfast time, when I would run down to the gate to meet her so that I could wheel her

Even now I can picture him standing at the end of the path, unbuckling his belt and shouting that he would teach me manners if it was the last thing he did. I fled then, out of the garden gate and down the Drift, and when I plucked up the courage to return, the incident was not mentioned.

'My father never raised a hand to anyone in his life,' my mother told me. 'We all did bicycle up the path and into the shed. Then I would follow her into the house and we would have breakfast with Aunt Norah and whoever else was staying at the time. Now there was a new inhabitant in the neighbourhood, brought into the world, as most babies seem to prefer, in the early hours of the morning. She would speak briefly about it to my aunt, but if she saw me taking an interest would say, 'Hush, little pitchers have big ears.'

I was too young to notice that she was tired, often exhausted, but Aunt Norah would fuss round her. As soon as we had finished breakfast Grandma would get up to clear the table, but Aunt Norah would tell her, 'I'll do that. Do you go and lie down.' To us she would say, 'Go and play somewhere quietly. Go for a long walk 'til dinner time.' We knew there was no point in hanging about the house, so we would take ourselves off down the Drift. By the time we returned, Grandma would be cheerfully cooking the dinner as if she had not been awake and working most of the night.

No one could remember, least of all Grandma herself, when she had first gone to a sick bed, or which had been her first confinement, but it is a fairly safe bet that it was a neighbour who needed help. Most likely it was one of her friends who knew how good she had been when her own baby daughter had been very ill and that she had assisted at the removal of my Uncle Arthur's tonsils on the kitchen table when he was a toddler and had not balked at the sight of blood. 'Weren't you frightened?' I asked her when she told me about that. 'I didn't have time to be afraid. I hatta scrub the table and get hot water and soap and then help with the anaesthetic and hold the light for the doctor to see what he was a-doin.' White-faced and white-aproned, she must have been trembling to start with, but the doctor would not have allowed her to let the light waver. He would have had no patience with fainting fits or hysterics. Besides, Eliza was wise enough to know she was needed; she forced herself to be practical and because she stayed cool and did as she was instructed, the operation was a complete success.

However she got started, the word soon spread that she was competent, willing and cheerful and, besides that, did not charge the earth, and before long she was in great demand. Live births, still births, easy births and difficult ones, boys, girls and twins; they were all part of a day's – or a night's – work for her. The father or an older child would come down the Drift to fetch her and, if it was the middle of the night, would throw pebbles at her bedroom window. When Grandad got up and put his head out, he would be greeted with, 'Mr Ong, will you ask Mrs Ong to come.' On one occasion, the urgency was stressed by the added, 'She be hully diluted', meaning fully dilated, and Eliza would dress and go.

Over her dress she wore a sparkling white apron, which she pinned up at the corners to keep the inside pristine until she arrived at her destination. She carried a black bag into which she put the things she might need, such as swabs, disinfectant and mild painkillers. They did not have analgesics in the early days and none were expected. The mother-to-be would already have been given a list of things to have ready, such as torn up sheets for draw sheets and pads, old newspapers, boiling water, a small bath, carbolic soap and the baby's crib, or a suitable drawer, and clothes to dress the infant in. My grandmother would duplicate some of these in her bag in case they were not ready.

If the baby was a first one, she might find the young husband in a panic and have to calm him down before she could do anything. This was usually achieved by giving him something positive to do, such as stoking up the fire and putting the kettle and a saucepan of water on to boil. The bed would be stripped of its usual sheets and blankets and freshly laundered ones put in their place over lots of padding. No one wanted to spoil the mattress, which would have been an expensive item in a poor home. There was no electricity so that at night the only light to work by came from oil lamps and candles, even in the more well-to-do homes.

Grandma never refused to attend, even when she knew she would not be paid. In any case she had no fixed rate of payment. When her patients asked what they owed, she would say, 'Give me what you can afford.' In the early days she would be offered a shilling, half a crown, perhaps ten shillings, very occasionally a whole pound, and that would probably be for twins. When the family was large and she went year after year, the mother would sometimes miss paying her one year and pay double the next, when perhaps her circumstances had improved.

A couple of Grandma's notebooks have survived in which she wrote down the name of the patient and in the case of a birth, the sex of the infant and the payment she received. One of the little books lists some 44 cases, including four sets of

A page from one of Eliza's notebooks in which she kept a record of the births she attended and how much she was paid.

twins and one still birth. The most she was paid in those years was £1 7s 6d[1] for delivering a baby girl. One entry has a dash beside it, which probably means she worked for nothing. Village surnames like Powley, Yaxley, Ellis, Green and Hubbard appear over and over again. On another tiny scrap of paper, which is gnawed by mice, she listed ten births in three months, none of them in Necton, so it seems she kept a separate record for those that took place outside the village. If you asked her why she did it, she would shrug her shoulders and quote:

[1] 1 shilling is equivalent to 5p; half a crown, or 2s. 6d. is 12p; 5s is 25p, 10s is 50p and 2.4d is 1p.

Mrs. H. Waters, Necton. 7th Daughter. April 12th.

Miss. Mann. Edw. St. Swaffham. 4½ Son. April. 20th.

Mrs. Ligh. pool. Swaffham. (8) Daughter. April. = 19th

Mrs. Knock. Man St. = 7 Son. May. 1st.

X Mrs Sebbingo Holme 6½ Son June. 3rd X.

Mrs. Barber. London. St. Swaffham. 9½ Son. June. 7th

Mrs. Winns Beacham well. 6¾ Son June 8th

Mrs. Mindam Holme Hale (stillborn) girl. June. 14th

Mrs. Parker, Sporle (Stillborn) Boy, 6lb. June 16th

Mrs. Rowe, Little Dunham. girl. 8lb. June. 22th.

The piece of paper noting 10 births outside Necton, the weight and sex of the baby, and the date of birth.

> Do the work that's nearest
> Though it's dull at whiles
> Helping, when you meet them,
> Lame dogs over stiles.

There was hardly a family in the village untouched by her ministrations, either at confinement, convalescence, illness, injury or death; they all knew her capable manner and gentle touch. She became known as the Mother of Necton, uninfluenced by the machinations of the nursing world, which was striving to do away with the unqualified midwife.

At the beginning of the century, the uncertificated woman who served a village community in this way was referred to as the handywoman or 'the woman you sent for'. If you were lucky, she was clean and knowledgeable and could tell at a glance whether it was going to be necessary for a doctor to attend. You only sent for the doctor when you were ill and childbirth was not an illness. Besides, doctors cost money and the village midwife charged only a minimal fee. She was as necessary to village life in those early days as the blacksmith, the miller and the horse doctor. These women were often derided as Sarah Gamps by those lucky enough to have been able to qualify, but that was unfair on many of them. Certainly no one could have been more careful or caring than my grandmother, whose standard of cleanliness was very high indeed.

The Midwives' Institute, later to become the Royal College of Midwives, had been founded to ensure that all women, whatever their status, had access to a qualified midwife and doctor. It wanted to stamp out the Sarah Gamps, believing them to be dirty and ignorant and doing more harm than good, even if they were well-meaning. In some cases, this was undoubtedly true, but like all sweeping generalisations, it ignored the dedicated, experienced midwife who had been doing the job for years. In many cases she was the only source of help to some women, mainly because qualified midwives had to be paid commensurate with their status, but also because they were not often on the spot in rural areas.

The scheme was dogged by administrative wrangles: what training the nurse should have; what she should wear; whether she should have a donkey and cart, a pony and trap or should be provided with a bicycle to get about her district; what she should be paid and how the money was to be found; whether she should live in a house provided for her or have a living out allowance; what her duties should and should not entail. 'A lot o' squit,'[2] Grandma said. 'You just hatta get on with the job and do your best.'

In 1887, money collected from the women of Britain to commemorate Queen Victoria's Golden Jubilee had been used to set up a system of district nursing all over the country. Suitable women were selected from towns and villages and sent for training, at the end of which they went back to practice what they had learned. They were called Jubilee nurses. But in rural areas, their introduction was slow, mainly because of the difficulty of covering scattered country communities and organising sufficient supervision, and the fund rapidly ran out of money.

In 1902, a little before my grandmother began practising, the First Midwives' Act had set up the Central Midwives Board to regulate training and examinations and issue or cancel certificates. Local Supervisory Authorities were set up to keep a list of practising midwives in their area, ensuring they knew the regulations. Their remit also included investigating malpractice and, where necessary, suspending midwives from working in the interests of maintaining hygiene and preventing infection. Puerperal infection was the scourge of childbirth in those early days and many women died of it, even after a successful delivery.

Three years later, the first Roll of Midwives was published. It contained the names of those who already had a midwifery qualification from a recognised body and those who had passed a CMB examination. Because their numbers were small and they were mostly concentrated in towns, the list also contained the names of those women of good character who had been in practice for at least a year and whose competence was vouchsafed by the local general practitioner. These were called 'bona fide' midwives. Unfortunately, there are no records of these women and so I do not know if my grandmother was one of them. From then on, no one could call herself a midwife unless she had a certificate. The 'woman you sent for' was supposed to 'assist', by doing the washing and housework and looking after the rest of the family, leaving the midwife free to attend to the patient.

This did not work either; there were too few certified midwives to go round and the country people still preferred their old meth-

[2]nonsense

ods. Patients would often engage a doctor whom they knew was willing to work with the local handywoman because he would accept a low fee, knowing he would not be called in except as an emergency.

In 1910 the government had decreed that women who were not certified could not attend a childbirth, 'habitually and for gain', except under the direction of a medical practitioner. All of this washed over the head of my grandmother, who had a family of her own to look after and could not have left home to do the required training. She had two tutors: her own experience of life and the instruction of the doctors with whom she worked and who trusted her implicitly and recommended her to their patients, even when there was a qualified midwife available.

'If we saw Granny Ong trotting up the road carrying her bag, we'd look at each other and say, "So and so must be going to have her baby."' Dolly Bell, daughter of my grandmother's close friend, Maud Powley, told me. 'And a little while later, we'd see her come back and we'd call out, "Is she all right? What did she have?" and Granny Ong would smile and say, "A little boy, both doing well." And on she'd go. Or it might be a girl, or twins. But she never said anything else, not about the case. That was confidential and one thing you could be sure of with Mrs Ong was that she'd keep a confidence.'

Grandma could hold her tongue, could smile secretly to herself, knowing the truth and not feel the need to broadcast the fact, which is a virtue not many of us have. She must have known all sorts of things about the lives of the villagers, but try and draw her out and all you would

get was, 'I don't know anything about such things.'

Contraception was rarely used and many women relied on a sponge soaked in vinegar. Some, too desperate to think of the consequences, tried to induce abortions with large doses of gin and nutmeg or herbal concoctions recommended by well-meaning friends, often with near-fatal results. Grandma shut her eyes to it all and never gossiped, but I was told by someone else that she had threatened one woman who had dosed herself so often to 'get rid of it' that she would not attend her if she did it again. She was not taking the moral high-ground, but simply thinking of the health of the mother and the welfare of the existing children. Nor do I think she would have carried out her threat.

Grandma moved promptly and efficiently when things went wrong. With no formal training, she had an unerring instinct that told her what to do and when to send for a doctor, and that was not done lightly when doctor's fees took some finding. She mourned with a family when a baby died and many a time she saved both mother and child when both seemed lost. She was skilful, sympathetic and impossible to shock, never showing by the slightest change in her expression, either doubt or revulsion.

Not only did my grandmother bring people into the world, she helped ease their way out of it too, if that was all that there was left to do. Leaving a warm bed and her own healthy family, she would sit, hour after hour, watching a life ebb away, ministering gently and listening to the incoherent words of someone slipping from this world into the next. She must have learned some long-kept secrets at these times, but she never spoke of them.

In those days, even if someone died in hospital, they were taken home before the funeral so that family and friends could pay their last respects. Grandma would wash them and lay them out ready for the family to view before the funeral. Often she would help with the funeral tea, making sandwiches and scones and lending her treasured china tea set.

That was why we grandchildren were sent away to play on some days when she had to catch up on her sleep, but we were soon chatting together in companionship again, though she never spoke to me of her work; that came later when I was grown up. She was never too busy to listen to tales of childish doings, to explain mysteries that seemed insoluble to a seven-year-old, to talk of her childhood, the years in which she grew up and married, the hardships she endured, to inculcate in me her own conviction of what was right and proper, her strong sense of duty, her unfailing humour.

'That time o' day', she would begin. She was not referring to the hours and minutes, but simply reminiscing about times gone by and when she said it, I knew there was another of her nostalgic stories coming and I would lean forward expectantly. I had a glimpse of my mother's childhood through those stories and I knew, hard though it had been, it had been a happy one.

The Early Years

M Y GRANDMOTHER was born Eliza Marie Brown, the eldest child of John and Elizabeth Brown. John, who had followed the family tradition and was a brickmaker, was the eldest son of James and Sarah Brown. James and his growing family had moved from Heacham to Fakenham in the early 1870s and it was in Fakenham that John met Elizabeth Crockley, daughter of William and Eliza Crockley. They were married in 1880 and set up their home in Holt. Eliza was born on 29 May 1882.

Soon after Eliza's birth, the little family moved back to Fakenham where Sarah Elizabeth was born in 1885. She was followed by Alice Victoria in April 1887, much to the chagrin of her father who was disappointed at not being able to produce a son. Soon after this, James Brown left Fakenham to set up in business in Necton, but John and Elizabeth and their three little girls did not go with them. They moved to Swaffham where John obtained employment.

It was in Swaffham that Eliza went to the National School, dressed in stiff cotton skirts down to her ankles, a white starched apron and black button boots. Her education cost a begrudged penny a week, which she was given every Monday to take with her. According to her own account she sometimes appropriated the penny for sweets – you could buy quite a lot for a penny – and because she dare not arrive at school without the coin, she played hooky, hiding behind the gravestones in the churchyard until all the other children had gone into school. She never said what punishment she received for this; it might not have been considered a serious crime to skip school, but the theft of the penny certainly would have been. That was one thing I appreciated about my grandmother, she never pretended she had always been good and I enjoyed hearing that she was sometimes naughty.

'We were no different from other children,' Grandma said. I was helping her wash up at the time. This was done on the kitchen table with a bowl and a tin tray as a draining board. Grandma washed and I dried, putting the things carefully in their appropriate places in the cupboards when I had done so. 'We hatta work and work hard but we have[3] our fun and games too. There were hoops, of course, and we bowl them along the road and have races. If we manage to get hold of an iron one instead of a wooden one, we were in clover. You could let your friends borrow it for an aniseed ball or a marble. Bowling hoops was always followed by hopscotch, then tops. They were made of wood and painted in bright colours. There was a proper season for everything. Later we hev skipping and sing rhymes while we did it. And we play with marbles and five stones.' She smiled at me,

[3]The past tense in the Norfolk vernacular is often ignored and though it is easy to follow in speech it can be confusing when written down. I have used it sometimes because that was how my grandmother spoke.

hands deep in sudsy water, 'Not so very different from now, is it?'

In 1887, to mark Queen Victoria's Golden Jubilee, Eliza and her sister, Sarah, joined the rest of the poorer inhabitants of Swaffham in the celebrations on Market Hill, where tables for dinner were set out in the street. When the adults had finished their meal, the children were given a tea of bread, butter and jam, with cakes and lemonade. Afterwards there was a firework display. 'Some on 'em et too much and got sick,' she told me, 'but it were a grand day. We didn't get too many of those.'

Before Sarah was old enough to join Eliza at school and while Alice was still a toddler, their mother became pregnant again. The pregnancy did not go smoothly and Elizabeth was frequently tired. Eliza found herself more and more often acting 'mother' to her two young sisters. When Grandmother Brown arrived on a visit and saw what was happening, she offered to take two-year-old Alice back to Necton with her. Eliza, aged seven, and Sarah, aged four, were considered old enough to look after themselves and help their mother, and Grandmother Brown's house was already bursting at the seams, so only one could go.

When her mother's labour began, it was Eliza who fetched the midwife. She stayed home from school that day in case she was needed to run errands and also to make meals for her father and Sarah. The labour was a difficult and messy one and Eliza was undoubtedly aware of what was happening, even if she was not in the room. It had a profound effect on her young mind and the way she viewed childbirth in later years. The baby, a fourth girl, was born on 30 April 1890 and was named Maria.

Elizabeth never got out of bed again; she died exactly two weeks later, probably of puerperal fever, and the little family was bereft. It seemed to eight-year-old Eliza that the world had come to an end.

The funeral service was short and Elizabeth Brown, aged only 36, was laid to rest in an unmarked grave in a corner of Swaffham churchyard. Eliza always said she could pick out the exact spot even without a stone. It may have accounted for her insistence on buying some sort of urn or stone to mark every family grave afterwards, even when she could ill afford it.

Left to raise his girls single-handed and without the son he longed for, John did not seem able to cope. Alice stayed at Necton and Eliza found herself trying to look after her father, five-year-old Sarah and the baby. In her own words, she 'didn't think much to that', an understatement if ever there was one. John decided there was nothing for it but to invite another woman into his home.

Annie Stevens, a year younger than Eliza's mother had been, was designated housekeeper. Eliza was relieved of some, but not all, of her household chores and sent back to school before the attendance officer arrived on their doorstep. But she was deeply traumatised at the loss of her beloved mother and hated to see the new housekeeper using her mother's things, possibly even sleeping in her bed, and telling her what she should and should not do. The poor woman was probably trying to do her best for the young family, but Eliza saw her as a usurper. She played truant more often and hiding among the gravestones took on a deeper meaning.

Matters came to a head in the summer of

1891. Her father, miserable and frustrated, chastised her once too often and Eliza decided to run away from home. Taking nothing with her, she walked the four miles to Necton to put her case to Grandmother Brown.

The brickmaker's premises were on the Dereham Road, between the Necton cross roads and Little Fransham. Built in 1864 of red brick and flint, the house was really a double dweller,[4] but the family was so big that it occupied the whole building. In an arched niche in the middle of the façade was a statue of a boy holding a bird's nest. The statue was probably made by the brickmakers themselves, who often included stonemasonry among their talents. The strange thing about the statue was that it had been made with a hand missing. The boy had fallen from a tree while raiding birds' nests and had broken his arm so badly that it had to be amputated. The statue was meant as a dreadful warning to any child who dared to rob the birds of their eggs. Grandma had a rhyme about it:

> The robin and the red breast
> The robin and the wren
> If ye take out of their nest,
> Ye'll never thrive again.
> The robin and the red breast
> The martin and the swallow
> If ye touch one o' their eggs
> Bad luck will surely follow.

That statue stood in its niche for over 100 years, until the two houses were made into one. Then the alcove became the front porch and the statue was put into the front garden. My grandmother always spoke nostalgically of it, but she was not thinking

The house at the brickworks with the statue of the one-armed boy standing in its niche.

about the statue when she knocked on the door on that autumn day in 1891.

Though of average height for her age, she was thin and pale and shabbily dressed, for Annie Stevens was not so careful of the children's appearance as their mother had been. She had been crying and the tears had made streaks down her grubby cheeks so that she looked a truly pathetic figure. Her grandparents took her in, cleaned her up and gave her a meal while she declared firmly that she was never going back. They must have understood how the child felt because they agreed she could stay with them, envisaging no argument from their son who would undoubtedly be glad to have another of his daughters off his hands. But there was one condition. There were already too many mouths to feed who were not yet old enough to contribute to the weekly budget, so Eliza must earn her keep working in the brickyard and they would give her 1 shilling a week for herself.

[4] A double dweller is a pair of semi-detached houses.

There were, living at the brickworks at that time, James and Sarah, their daughter Maria, sons Benjamin and Walter, grandson Alfred, then 15, who was already working in the brickyard, and a new grandson, Percy, as well as Eliza's sister, Alice. Benjamin was the only one who had not followed the brickmaking trade and was a farm labourer. How many other employees there were, I do not know.

'What about school?' Eliza ventured, perking up at the prospect of escaping her chores at home, not realising she would be exchanging one kind of drudgery for another. 'No more school for you,' her grandfather said, and he was right; she never went to school again. She could read and write quite well, better than some of the adults around her, and she could add and subtract and handle money and that was considered education enough. She should have taken an educational test and been issued with a labour certificate before starting work, but it was unlikely she had reached the required standard by this age, although some bright children did manage to convince the authorities they were 'educated' by the time they were 11 or 12 years old and were allowed to leave school.

Her grandparents must have told her that if anyone came asking questions, she was to say she was 13 and she was to stick to that however hard she was pressed, because otherwise she would be sent back to her father and everyone would be in dire trouble. So Eliza added four years to her age and never told a soul, sticking to that lie throughout her long life, destroying anything in the way of papers or photos that might give the game away. Even her marriage certificate, the earliest document relating to her own life to survive, has the wrong age on it. I would be surprised if my grandfather had not known he was ten rather than six years older than Eliza, but Alice, her sister, grew up believing there were more years between them than there really were.

My grandmother must have been a very young looking 13, and one can only suppose that no attendance officer appeared in those early years, or he would surely have been suspicious. Hard work and better food soon put some flesh on her as she was forced to leave her childhood behind and grow up. Childhood games were forgotten as she set to work learning the business of brickmaking.

Before the coming of the railways, most small towns and large villages had brickworks, often as a sideline to farming, based at the nearest pit where suitable clay could be extracted. Bricks were always wanted for dwellings, farm buildings, breweries, maltings, warehouses and suchlike, so there was a steady demand and brickmaking was a fairly sure means of making a living. The bricks were transported to their destination by horse and cart and so it was sensible for builders to buy locally and keep transport costs to a minimum.

The advent of railways meant that the bricks still had to be taken to the railway terminal in the time-honoured way, but once there, they could be sent almost anywhere. This was both a curse and a blessing. In the late 19th century the entrepreneurial Victorians embarked on expansion and fuelled a demand for bricks for churches, chapels, schools, hospitals, town halls, public houses and railway stations. For a time, brickmaking flourished.

The Brown brickworks occupied three acres of land not far from the house and close to a large clay pit. As soon as breakfast was over, Eliza put on a huge sacking apron that came down to her boots, covered her hair with a mob cap and accompanied the menfolk down to the pit to help shift the clay, known as 'gault', as it was dug from the pit and piled up for the winter frosts to break it up.

Digging was seasonal, starting in autumn and continuing until February and that year's digging had just begun. The piles of clay were turned periodically and this must have been a back-breaking job. I doubt whether Eliza was expected to do this, but there were other things she could do. 'The actual brickmaking began in the spring,' she told me. 'The clay had to be puddled.'

'What's that mean?' We were sitting outside the back door, side by side, stripping blackcurrants for jam. My hands were purple with their juice, but I was so interested in her story I did not even notice.

'It hatta be wetted and stirred up to make it like dough,' she said. 'In early times it was done by workers treading it and turning it with spades, but by the time I start work it was put in a pug mill, that's a kind of barrel with an upright shaft down the middle and sharp blades sticking out. It was worked by a horse harnessed to a beam attached to the shaft. I hatta lead the horse round and round and that turn the blades.'

'Then what?'

'There were other things add to get rid of impurities and make exactly the right kind of mix. It was like making a giant cake with a secret recipe. Then the mixture was shaped into bricks by a machine that cut and grind the clay and then force it out through a hole the shape of a brick, so it come out like toothpaste. It were cut into separate bricks by wires on a frame,' She smiled. 'Do you know why a brick is the size it is?'

'No.'

'It's the size of a man's hand, so he can pick it up easily. The clay were pressed into a mould and levelled off using a stick called a strike. The bricks just out o' the mould were called green bricks 'cos they hadn't been fired. We spread them on a flat wheelbarrow and took them to the drying ground. We arranged them in a herringbone pattern on wooden racks, row on row, up to 10ft high. The stack was called a hack and we leave this to cure, which mean dry enough to be fired. We start firing in April and it go on all summer, until all the clay was used up and we hatta start digging more.'

'What was the kiln like?'

'It were like a big oven with holes along the bottom for the fuel and an opening opposite the holes called a wicket. There were more holes at the top and that control the air that make the fire burn. The fire were lit at the bottom and the heat gradually draw up through the bricks. Stacking the bricks in the kiln were a skilled job and I was never let do it, though I watched it done many a time. You hatta do it so not too many were spoiled by under or over burning.'

'The fire was let burn slow for three days and then we open the fire holes and took off the roof to let more air in and make it burn faster. After a two or three days fast burning, all the holes were blocked up and the fire let burn itself out. The bricks were real hot, so we hatta let them cool for another week before we could take them out. Then we got the kiln ready for the next batch.'

Early fuel was ling (heather), furze (gorse) or bracken. By my grandmother's time they were using coal, though furze and bracken were still used to light the fire and it was one of her tasks to collect it. 'Kissing's out of season when the gorse is not in bloom,' she told me, explaining, when I asked her what she meant, that it was an old saying meaning that kissing was never out of season because there is always some blossom on the gorse bush whatever the time of year. 'It were very prickly,' she said. 'I were forever pulling needles out o' my fingers, even though I wore thick gloves.'

Her work was dirty and physically demanding, but she stuck it out. She was earning her keep and a tiny wage besides, and it was better than being at Swaffham with her father and Annie Stevens. So she went on carrying green bricks to the kiln and fired bricks to the stacks to be sent to their customers, throwing out those that were too burned and those that were not burned enough, shaping bricks, stacking bricks, fetching brushwood, and leading the horse in its endless perambulation, working from six in the morning to six in the evening. She became strong and sturdy and independent.

Eliza was very close to her younger sister, Alice. They had shared so much sorrow and now they were coming out of it in the good-natured shambles of life with the Brown tribe. Alice went to school, ignorant of the fact that her sister should have been going with her.

Working outside in the summer was one thing, working outside in the winter, when feet became numb and hands chapped with being continually wet, was quite another. But Eliza, stubbornly determined, would not complain. The winter of 1894 was a particularly hard one. The pit from which the clay was dug was too frozen to work, but if they could not work, they could play. Wrapped in coats and scarves, they enjoyed themselves, slipping and sliding over the ice on the local ponds, laughing and screaming when they fell. Eliza pulled Alice along on a makeshift sled until their cheeks glowed and their eyes sparkled like the frost all round them.

Eliza was still little more than a child. Her personality was a bewildering mixture of worldliness and innocence. She was expected to do the labour of a grown woman and to stick to the task in hand without distractions, yet she had the lively spirit and enquiring mind of a child and hard work never quelled her enthusiasm for enjoyment. Necton became home and if she ever wondered what had become of her father and other two sisters, she did not dwell on it. Nor did she trouble herself pondering on what the future might hold for her. Little girls of ten, even those pretending to be fourteen, are not usually given to dreams of what might have been or what could be.

In 1897, like everyone else, the girls joined in the celebrations for Queen Victoria's Diamond Jubilee and, as for the Golden Jubilee ten years before, there were tea parties and dancing and flag-waving, and commemorative mugs for the children. But for the Brown family it was a time of change.

More advanced brickmaking machines were coming into use about that time: mechanical presses, machines for making holes through the bricks, and revolutionary kiln design, but James could not afford them. He was feeling the pinch of competition with the big concerns who had more mechanisation and could produce bricks in larger quantities, which were then carried by rail a much greater distance. He could not supply bricks in enough quantity, and when the clay ran out another source had to be found. James was nearly 70 and decided the time had come to cut his losses and retire.

The boys could make their own way and find themselves jobs, but Eliza and Alice were a problem. Their father, who had enough on his plate with his two other daughters, had shown little interest in them since they had been living with their grandmother, besides I do not think Eliza would have wanted to return to him. She was 13, pretending to be 17, and she had to be found a job where she could live in, but Alice was only nine, and after much debate it was decided to send her to a church home in Leicester.

The parting of the sisters was a tearful one, but they promised to write to each other and did so regularly for the rest of

The Three Tuns public house.

their lives. Leicester seemed like the end of the earth to the little girl, who must have felt lonely and abandoned. But there was nothing Eliza could do to help her. Her own future was being decided.

Eliza, with little say in the matter herself, became a housemaid to Mr and Mrs Benstead who kept the Three Tuns public house, which stood on the crossroads where the road from Swaffham to East Dereham met the road from Necton to Dunham. Mrs Benstead was no more unkind than other employers of domestic labour. She treated her servant as she thought servants should be treated, with strict rules and firm discipline.

Her days in service were no more nor less full than they had been at the brickyard, but the jollity went out of them. There was no family feeling, and though the Browns were less than half a mile away, time off was rare and she had no one with whom to share a joke or a problem. Eliza accepted that she could not turn the clock back and that the best thing she could do was to grin and bear it and look forward to her limited time off.

'Five o'clock in the morning, I hatta get up,' my grandmother told me, though that was hardly different from when she was working in the brickyards. 'I hatta clean out the range in the kitchen, then black lead it and polish it until you could see your face in it, and then polish the brass rail that run round the top of the fender. When I had done that, I brung in the sticks and coal and light the fire so that it was hot for cooking the breakfast when Mrs Benstead got up.' It was while bringing in the coals that Eliza fell and gashed her shin on the newly-blacked fender. It was a bad cut and being so close to the bone, bled profusely. 'It's not that bad,' Mrs Benstead said when she inspected the injury. 'Clean it up and bandage it before it ruins the rug and then get on with your work.' No sympathy there, though the injury was painful.

That, my grandmother told me, was how she came to have an ulcer on her leg, which remained there until the day she died. I suspect some of the cleaning fluid they used for the range got into the wound. Sometimes it would heal up for a bit, but the slightest knock would open it again and she always wore a protective crêpe bandage. Every night she would unravel it from her leg, roll it up methodically and put it on the bedside table beside the candle and alarm clock. Every morning before putting her feet to the floor, she neatly bandaged her leg again.

After breakfast there was the rest of the house to clean and the bar to sweep and dust. There were no domestic appliances, of course. Salt was used to clean the scum from the bath and stale bread to clean wallpaper. Tea leaves were sprinkled on the carpets before sweeping them with a broom. I do not know if this was supposed to aid in the cleaning process or was simply done to lay the dust and stop it flying on to furniture, pictures and ornaments, but even when I was at Necton, many years later, my grandmother sprinkled old tea leaves on the carpet in the sitting room before attacking it with a broom and a brush and dustpan.

Stone steps were cleaned to pristine whiteness with a mixture of pipe clay, lime and stone blue, boiled together and used when cold. When this dried, the steps were brushed and rubbed with a piece of flannel and woe betide any tradesman who dared to walk on them immediately after they had been done. She did not go to bed until the last piece of crockery had been washed up from the last meal of the day and all the used glasses in the bar had been washed, polished and replaced on the shelves.

Eliza was 14, but calling herself 18 and, by now, the four-year gap was hardly noticeable. For all her hard work she was fast growing into a beautiful woman, with a classically oval face, luxuriant warm brown hair and mischievous blue eyes that never lost their sparkle. She had a good figure and carried herself with a poise that was unusual for one in her situation. There were many admiring glances from the young men in the village, among whom was Walter Ong, a friend of her uncle, Benjamin. Eliza liked him, but she was not at that time thinking of courtship or marriage. Work filled her days.

The Ongs

THE ONGS had been in Necton village since the middle of the 18th century, descended from Daniel Onge and his wife, Margaret. They had an enormous family, many of whom died very young. Of the four surviving sons, three remained in Necton and had families of their own, now called Ong without the 'e'. It has been suggested that the name is a corruption of Owen or Ewin, or perhaps Wang, an old English word meaning meadow land. Another theory is that it is a misspelling of the Scandinavian prefix Ing, which was the theory my Uncle Arthur favoured.

He believed that our ancestor was a Scandinavian seafaring man who jumped ship at King's Lynn and walked inland, determined to put as much distance as possible between himself and his ship before he was missed. Somewhere in Norfolk he settled, married and founded a family with its roots firmly in the soil and not a drop of sea water in its blood. I am not sure I agree, but it is a romantic idea.

My grandfather was born on 23 January 1872, the sixth child and second son of David and his wife, Sarah. Two of their children, Elizabeth, age four, and Emma, aged six months, had died within two days of each other 10 months before Walter was born. What had carried them off, I do not know, but undoubtedly it was an infection of some sort, perhaps 'flu or scarlet fever. Of the surviving children, the oldest was Charles, eight years Walter's senior; Hannah who was four years older than Walter; another Elizabeth who was three years younger; Arthur, born in 1881 and

David Ong, Walter's father.

Sarah Ong, Walter's mother.

expression, though I have been told he was a kindly man. His wife was plump and rather heavily featured; she wore her hair scraped back in a bun and dressed severely, mostly in black. She was, I am told, a tartar and ruled the family with a rod of iron. David had been a farm labourer all his working life and until 1892 was working at Ivy Todd farm and living in a tied cottage. Charles, his eldest son, joined him as a labourer as soon as he was old enough.

The year of 1879, when Walter was only seven, was a disastrous one and began the long depression in Norfolk farming that lasted on and off until World War I. Farms became neglected and overgrown. Much that had once been ploughed and producing crops was allowed to lie fallow and became meadow land. But this meadow land could support cattle and sheep and men skilled in working with animals were more secure than general farm labourers.

Day labourers were given trivial stop gap jobs around the farmhouse if the farmer could afford to pay them, otherwise they were laid off and with no unemployment benefits, many found it almost impossible to provide their families with food. Poaching was rife and severely dealt with. Many, who feared the gamekeeper, were reduced to catching and eating sparrows.

I was horrified at the idea of eating these tiny birds, but my grandmother assured me it was true. 'The men used to go out at night with a big net and a lantern,' she said. 'They hang the netting over the hedge, or a straw stack if they thought the birds had settled into one, and then shine the lantern into it, which confused the birds and they'd fly into the net. They'd trap a score or more at a time.'

Florence, the baby of the family, born in 1886 when her mother was 45. There were 22 years between the first child and the last.

Pictures of David show him to have been a sturdy man with a dark beard and a dour

'Then what?'

'They brung 'em home and their women skin 'em and open up the breasts and boil them in a pan to make a stew.'

'But wasn't it full of bones?'

'Bless you, course it was. You just hatta pick them out. They made a nourishing meal when there was no meat to go on the table.'

It was at this desolate time that many of the young single men left the area to look for employment in the 'sheres', meaning the counties to the west and north, rather than take parish relief. Charles left home to the lure of industrial wages in the Midlands. He found work in an iron foundry in Middlesbrough and sent a little money home to his family every week.

Their lives revolved around the farming year, the ploughing, the lambing, hay making and harvest, bad summers and good summers, severe winters, droughts and disastrous floods. School was purely incidental.

Because of the Education Act of 1870, when education became compulsory, Walter had been enrolled at the village school, founded by the Squire of Necton in 1889, but his attendance record was abysmal and he never learned to read and write properly. His poor attendance was not due to idleness or a reluctance to learn, but simply because he was needed to work alongside his father, especially with so many girls in the family. Until they were ready to go into service or marry, they had to be provided for. Nor was he unique; headmasters frequently complained that the Attendance Officer could get no response from parents and that letters of warning, even supposing they could be read, went straight into the fire. One poor

master wrote in his log, 'Compulsory education in this country is a farce.'

Children helped with the weeding and haymaking, picking potatoes and gathering acorns to feed the pigs, as well as bringing in the harvest. The harvest was the culmination of a year of toil, the time when all the watching of the weather and the speculation about the yield became fact and you learned whether you would be able to live comparatively comfortably for the next 12 months or whether you must pull in your belt another notch and hope for better times to come. Every able-bodied man, woman and child was expected to give a hand 'gaining' the harvest, even the inmates of the workhouse and unemployed labourers had work to do then. The long summer holiday from school was known as the harvest holiday and it could be brought forward if the corn ripened early or extended if the season was late. 'Gaining' the harvest was definitely more important than formal education.

Nonetheless, my grandfather was an astute man and not easy to fool. Few people, with the exception of my grandmother who knew how to go about it, ever attempted to pull the wool over his eyes. He could sign his name and had a cheque book that Grandma always filled in for him, but he would put his name to nothing until he knew exactly what he was signing. Patiently Grandma would say, 'Pa, use your eyes. Look, it say five pounds here in words and here it is in figures.' The figures he could read.

His comment when, in 1911, he was told he would have to pay a few pence National Insurance contributions each week was typical of him. '10 shillin' a week when I get to be 70,' he said, his voice heavy with sarcasm, 'and narthin' to dew, but sit on my arse all day. I'm fare gooin' to enjoy that, 'specially when I hatta pay for it now.'

In later years he would put a pair of metal-rimmed spectacles bought at Woolworth's on the end of his nose and pick out snippets from the newspaper. I can only surmise Eliza's patient tuition and a certain amount of pride had produced results.

In 1884, when he was twelve, Walter began work at Ivy Todd Farm as a back'us boy, which meant he was a general dogsbody under the thumb of the farmer's wife. His jobs were many and varied, from washing out the milking pails and taking them to the cowman, to cleaning out the grates, polishing boots and shoes, cleaning all the knives with bath brick and feeding the hens. He fetched the vegetables from the garden for the day's dinner, chopped wood, filled the coal scuttles and peeled the potatoes, jobs which were very little different from those Eliza had to do when she went to work at the Three Tuns. He had to dig the garden, run errands, or help unharness the horses. In fact anything and everything that other people wanted done. And for this he received the princely sum of 1s 6d a week.

There were perks, jobs for which he received extra payment, such as finding the hiding places of the hens and gathering their eggs, which earned him a penny a score, and plucking and drawing poultry just before Christmas, when there was a tremendous rush. That netted him twopence a bird. He also helped the shepherd at lambing time, for which he showed a particular aptitude.

He grew from what was designated half a man to a strong full-grown youth, able to do most of the jobs on the farm except pitching, for which the muscle and stamina of a full-grown man were needed, and that made him a three-quarter man in terms of wages. When the opportunity arose to assist the shepherd full-time, to become his 'page', he seized it eagerly. By learning to be a shepherd, he was ensuring a more stable future and a better wage than a general labourer. It was a generally held view that a labourer could master his trade by the time he was 21 and, unless he became a horseman, a shepherd or perhaps a foreman, there was no room for advancement. Walter needed to get on.

There is a saying that the churches of East Anglia are built on wool, though whether this is meant literally or figuratively is not clear. A great deal of money was donated to the churches by wealthy wool merchants of the 15th century when there was a spate of building and rebuilding; on the other hand, wool sacks were said to make good foundations, especially on marshy ground.

'The foot of the sheep turns the land to gold.' quoted my grandmother, steel needles clicking as she rapidly converted the product of that animal into a pair of thick socks for Grandad.

'What does that mean?' I asked her.

'Sheep feed the land with their droppings and the grease from their wool,' she explained, after she had laid her knitting against a completed sock and cocked her head sideways to see if she had reached the turning of the heel, 'and if you penned 'em close t'gether, they warmed it too. Then you move them on to the next bit. Then, in

June when they were sheared, you had their wool.'

Sheep, together with arable farming, continued to be the mainstay of life around Swaffham until well into this century. Walter became part of this tradition and carried his crook with pride. The first time he was entrusted to take a flock to Swaffham was a red letter day. He was up before dawn to muster the sheep and set them bleating and jostling along the narrow road from Necton to Swaffham; it needed all his attention and that of his hardworking dog, to keep them moving in the right direction. The dog, a cross between an old English sheep dog and a collie, was his constant companion. He was quick and intelligent and needed only the minimum in the way of command to know what do. 'He were a fare good dog,' he said. 'Didn't need no tellin'.'

He met more sheep as they passed the obsolete toll bar and rounded the bend by the ancient cedar tree on the outskirts of Swaffham. More flocks converged on the town from other directions until there were 3,000 of them bustling and bleating along the road towards the market, but careful shepherding kept them apart. Walter arrived in the market place just as his employer, with perfect timing, overtook him in his pony and trap to supervise the penning of the flock. Walter, together with a small band of boy volunteers anxious to make a penny or two, fetched the hurdles and mustered the sheep into groups of 20. They worked with a will and soon the Ivy Todd sheep had joined all the others, penned neatly in widely-spaced rows.

While they were waiting for the auctioneer to reach their sheep on his mobile rostrum – a four-wheeled farm cart – Walter was released to take in the sights. With the bleating of all those sheep, the barking of dogs and the chant of the auctioneers, the noise was almost deafening. In the side streets, stalls of goods had been set up to take advantage of the crowds and the money that was changing hands, and they did good business. Walter had a few coppers to spend and used them to good effect filling his stomach.

Suddenly there was a tremendous commotion in the middle of the market and everyone started running about and shouting, while loose sheep ran hither and thither in panic, determined to escape the noise for some peaceful meadow. Walter joined the chase and the sheep were soon safely inside the pens again. 'They wor whoolly[5] ras'less,' my grandfather said. 'It only tek one to git it into its head to be off, for the hull lot to imitate it. Norfolk sheep kin jump like stags, hurdles be narthin' but a short hop for 'em and once they git loose, there's no fixin' where they'll end up. You'd be searchin' the next shere.'

So Walter stood by as the auctioneer's cart made its way along the pens and stopped by his flock. There was a table on the cart and a clerk sat at this makeshift desk, writing down names and prices with a scratchy steel pen, while the auctioneer stood at the front pointing to the lot he was selling. He was a big man in breeches and bowler hat and he spoke so fast Walter could not altogether follow what he was saying, but in no time at all he had moved on and Walter's master touched him on the shoulder. 'Come you on, bor,[6] a quart of ale for me and a pint of beer for you and it's hoom for us and a good bargain struck.'

[5]wholely
[6]boy

They had a drink at the Horse and Groom and another at the Crown, once the town's coaching inn, before returning to Necton in the trap.

As he grew in stature and experience, Walter was entrusted to drive the sheep beyond Swaffham if the farmer thought he would get a better price at King's Lynn or Norwich. He would be two days on the road, spending the night in the hedge beside the meadow in which he had put the sheep for the night. When he went to Norwich, it was always the field next to Honington church. These fields were called night stances and the owner would charge so much per animal. The roads were narrow and winding and there was very little traffic on them, which was just as well – a hundred or more bleating sheep would certainly have caused problems.

Having sold his flock and with the proceeds safely tied round his waist in a body belt, he would have something to eat and drink before walking back with his dog, somewhat faster than he went. By the time he reached the crossroads at Necton, he had forgotten the drink he had had before setting out and turned in at the Three Tuns to 'wet his whistle'. He might also get a tantalising glimpse of the beautiful Eliza. He might even manage to speak to her and then he would return home happy.

All his sisters, except Florence, had left home and Arthur was not quite old enough

The Jolly Farmers (delicensed in 1910), known locally as the Black House, as it is today.

to begin work, so Walter continued to live at home and contribute to the family income. I doubt if marriage and setting up his own home ever entered his head, or if it did, was immediately banished as impossible.

In 1892, David Ong, as James Brown had done, decided the time had come to go in business on his own account. He took over the tenancy of the Jolly Farmers on the Holme Hale road, not far from the bottom end of Black Drift, combining it with a few acres of land that he farmed, most of it with barley. 'There were three kinds of beer,' my grandmother told me: 'best beer, that tasted like vinegar and was very strong; seconds, which was what you might call every day beer and small beer, which was weaker and was what the farm workers hev in the summer to slake their thirst.'

The house was a rambling building end on to the road with four labourers' cottages attached to it. There was a barn in the field behind it, which was the home of the Holme Hale witch: someone to strike terror into the hearts of small boys out after dark, especially at Halloween when witches were supposed to ride on broomsticks. Like all witches, she was consulted by ladies on affairs of the heart and anyone with a problem that needed supernatural powers to solve. Like many country people of that time, my great-grandparents believed in ghosts and the supernatural and would never have dreamed of deriding the power of the witches of this world, nor of evicting them from their land. She lived there unmolested. I suppose it was a kind of insurance policy against bad times. If so, it did not work.

The year 1894, produced a very bad harvest and there was heavy rain and flooding. Hay stood bedraggled and uncut, or if the farmer managed to get on the field in a dry spell to mow it, it lay about in blackened, sodden heaps, too wet to collect. The corn was slow in ripening and was so flattened that the primitive machinery could not cope with it when it was ready, so it had to be done by hand. Those whose holdings were small enough to be worked by the family and did not need to employ outside labour fared best, though even then it meant a great deal of tightening of belts. David Ong was beginning to regret his decision to go it alone, except that he could still sell beer – men needed something to relieve their misery – and Charles, still a bachelor at 30 years old, continued to send money home.

But worse was to come. In March 1895, David and Sarah received the devastating news from Charles' employers, Wilson and Co of the Tees Ironworks in North Ormesby, Middlesbrough, that their son had missed his footing while working at the summit of one of their kilns and had fallen into it, sustaining a fractured skull. He had been taken to the cottage hospital, where he was critically ill. The letter went on to say that everything possible was being done for him and they would be kept informed.

There followed an anxious week, in which David and Sarah hovered between optimism and despair and wondered if they could possibly afford the train fare to go and see him. Before they could make a decision on that, a second letter arrived, which regretted to have to inform them that Charles Ong had died of his injuries on 19

March and there would be an inquest. Not since they had lost their two daughters so tragically had they felt so bereft. Leaving his grieving family, David put on a suit and a collar and tie and caught a train to Middlesbrough to attend the inquest and arrange for his son's burial.

The inquest was held at the North Ormesby Cottage hospital where Charles had died. The coroner, a Mr Mackereth, called several of Charles's workmates to give evidence. One of them, who had been filling one of the kilns with calcined iron, testified that he had seen the deceased step from a gantry and fall into the kiln, a distance of some 35ft. Earlier in the day, some of his fellow workers had expressed surprise that three tipping holes – rather than the usual two – had been tapped into the kiln and they were sure Charles Ong had not noticed this. One of them said the first he knew of the accident was hearing another man call out, 'Charlie's gone!' and another said he was not sure if the deceased was aware of the third hole.

The coroner seemed very anxious to record a verdict of accidental death and David, listening to it and reading between the lines, felt that the management had been at fault and the coroner was aware of it. He became righteously indignant and went to see Wilson & Co., telling them that he laid the blame squarely at their door. They should not have sent Charles on to that platform without making sure he knew of the third hole in the kiln. He told them that Charles had been helping to maintain the family in very difficult times and without his contribution they would be in dire straits. They must have felt some measure of guilt because David was

awarded substantial compensation at a time when compensation for industrial injury was almost unheard of.

The wind was getting up as he boarded the train to return home and by the time he left it at Holme Hale station it was blowing with such ferocity, he could hardly stand against it. During the night it blew down scores of trees and whipped the roofs off houses and barns. And even worse, adding insult to injury, it blew the topsoil off the fields and along with it the newly-sown barley seed.

David had to sow the field again while trying to come to terms with the loss of his son and the grief of his wife, who was so overcome that she had little time for the surviving members of the family. Walter, who had remained at home and dutifully helped his father when not working at Ivy Todd Farm, could offer no comfort and indeed, his presence seemed to make matters worse and he mourned in private. But out of the tragedy, the fortunes of the Ongs took a turn for the better. David Ong put the compensation to good use.

Because of the low state of agriculture, farmers could not afford to pay their men except on a casual basis for haysel[7] and harvest. The ordinary day-to-day maintenance jobs had been neglected and in many cases the land itself had lost heart. The hedges grew untidily, the ditches were not cleaned out, thistles and nettles grew to gigantic proportions and idle machinery rusted in the barns. Many farmers were giving up altogether while others were reducing their holdings so that they need no longer employ labour. Some struggled on, hoping for improvement, waiting for just one harvest that would pay the bills and allow them to

[7] haymaking time

start the following season with a clean slate. A good summer was long overdue.

Farms were coming on to the market almost daily and at comparatively low prices; no one wanted to buy. It was in such a climate David Ong decided to take the biggest gamble of his life and go against the general trend. He gave up the tenancy of the Jolly Farmers and bought the small-holding in Black Drift, the place I knew so well as a child.

The independent smallholder worked longer hours than the average labourer and he had the additional concern of buying his own supplies, marketing his own produce and keeping his own books. His only employees were likely to be his children, who were often unpaid, being given spending money on an *ad hoc* basis. Making a living occupied his whole life. David Ong was no exception. He managed with the help of Arthur, now old enough to leave school, but it was decided imprudent for Walter to give up his job as a shepherd, so he worked all day for his master at Ivy Todd Farm and any spare time he had he helped his father. There was even less time to think of marriage, but his thoughts continually turned to Eliza. He was 25 years old and she was 15, though she was still maintaining the deception that she was four years older.

He was determined to find out how she felt about him and he did it in the time-honoured way on St Valentine's Day. He saved enough to buy a valentine card and attached it by a ribbon to an apple, which he had chosen carefully from a tray of them spread under his bed ever since the autumn before. Taking his missile, for missile it was meant to be, he walked across the fields to the brickworks, where he knew she was spending her afternoon off, and rapped smartly on the door. Then he nipped behind the nearest bush. When the door opened, he hurled the valentine into the hall and waited.

For a little while nothing happened – according to Grandma it did not do to appear too eager – but after a minute or two Eliza appeared on the step, looking out to see who her valentine might be. 'Who's there?' she called.

'Here,' he answered from the safety of the bush.

'Come you on out o' there,' she said, laughing.

He emerged and stood brushing his palms down his thick cord trousers and feeling foolish.

'Oh, it's you, Walter Ong,' she said. 'Now, what can you be wantin'?'

'Come for a walk.'

She laughed and pulled the door shut behind her. Their courtship had begun.

Looking Back

WALTER WAS considered a fine young man, with fair hair, grey-blue eyes and a moustache. Rough and ready he might have been, but he could be gentle and kind too, and Eliza, still very young, learned to love him. The seasons followed one upon the other, work crowded their days and the years passed without them being aware of their passing.

'There was allus more'n enough to do to keep us out o' mischief.' Grandma said. 'We both had to work long hours, none o' this beginning after breakfast and leaving off at teatime; we'd done half a day's labour by the time we stop for breakfast.'

We were sitting side by side peeling apples, she on a dining room chair, me on a little Windsor chair that was just the right size for little bottoms. She had a big enamel bowl full of cookers on her aproned lap and pared them swiftly and expertly with a little knife whose blade had been worn down by countless similar tasks. Its many sharpenings on the grindstone wheel, which stood in the garden, had reduced it to a small triangular sliver of steel on a wooden handle. She managed to produce a long corkscrew of thin peel, but mine came off in chunks, which wasted too much apple, and she stopped to show me how to do it.

'Blacking grates and scrubbing floors went on day after day, come what may. Grandad hev his job at Ivy Todd and he hatta help his father too, so we didn't see each other more'n a couple of times a week and then not for long. More often than not it was a quick cuddle behind the Tuns when I was supposed to be working.' The idea of Grandad cuddling Grandma amused me.

'Sometimes we'd go for a walk, but we didn't go far,' she went on, coring and cutting her apple into slices and plopping

Walter haymaking.

Eliza in the hayfield with little helpers from the village.

ing hens, fruit picking, egg gathering, haysel and harvest.'

I knew about haymaking because I had been on one of the meadows when the hay was raked up and loaded on to a haywain. It was almost as tall as a house and as wide as the lanes it traversed, so that the hedgerows of summer were garlanded with wisps of yellowing grass from its passing. We children would climb on top of it and sink back into the hay with the warm sun on our faces. Grandad would call, 'Howd yer!' meaning, 'hold on,' to those on top, but which the horse always took as a signal to move off, and we would be transported like a stately ship in full sail, from the field to wherever the stack was being built.

Before the tractor became commonplace, horses were the mainstay of the stock on any farm. They were sometimes great Clydesdales, but more often the sturdy, red-coated Suffolk Punch, which had a deep chest and short strong legs, ideal for pulling and they certainly had to do plenty of that. Horses pulled drills, harrows and reapers, water carts and haywains, besides those that were put in the shafts of carriages or used for riding.

They were often bred on the farm where they spent most of their working lives. A travelling hinksman[8] would lead a stallion into the village, its coat gleaming with health, its mane and tail brushed to shining glory with coloured ribbons in its harness and plaited into its hair. It was a marvellous sight as it plodded from farm to farm to serve the mares.

'Yer have to keep yar eye on 'em,' Grandad said, referring to the pregnant mares. 'They're not like sheep, you never know when they're going to drop their lit-

them into a bowl of salt water on the table at her side. She was going to make chutney and the onions would be the next for peeling and cutting up and then she would stop every now and again to wipe her streaming eyes. 'If we were late back we get a squaring up. We didn't have the freedom young people have nowadays.'

'What else did you do?' I asked, popping a piece of green peel into my mouth and chewing contentedly.

'There was plenty to do on the land, weeding and hoeing, not just in the garden but in the fields, hedging and ditching, looking after the sheep, milking cows, feed-

[8]The owner of a stallion used for breeding

tle 'uns. They'd fule you an' all if you watch 'em too close, pretendin' they got a long time to go and tellin' on you to go hoom to bed,' He saw me smile. 'You kin laugh, maw,[9] but hosses can talk if you've a mind to listen, but sometimes they tell falsehoods. Many a time I ha' gone to the stable of a mornin' and found a new foal and the mare lookin' like a dog with two tails.'

The horsemen were a breed apart, they imagined themselves a cut above the other farm workers and took a very real pride in the appearance of their charges, grooming them for hours after their normal working day was finished, training them, nursing them in sickness and even stealing linseed cake meant for the sheep, and oats from the milking cows, so that they would be extra well-fed and their coats glossy and smooth. It was a matter of pride to turn one's horses out to work in the fields as if they were about to enter the show ring.

The old smithy. Percy Lloyd was the blacksmith in the years before the war. Photo: Mrs Pauline Tenant

The harness, too, had to be looked after, the leather fed with oil and the brasses polished. Visits to the harness-maker and the blacksmith, next to the church, were made regularly. 'The smithy was the gossip shop of the village,' Grandma said with a smile.

'It were warm in there even on a bitter cold day with the doors wide open. The men would stand about while the smithy shoed their horses or repaired a farm implement they ha' brung him, and put the world to rights. It were fare better than the wireless for news.'

Of all the animals on the farm, I think my grandfather loved the horses the best. 'Yer know where yer are with a good hoss,' he would say. The pony, which pulled the trap, was his pride and joy and Grandma often said he loved 'that there animal' more than any human. I remember standing at a safe distance to watch him break in a pony. He had it in the orchard on a very long halter, guiding it clockwise round himself and talking to it for hours on end until it ceased to pull and answered to the lightest tug, then fed it with a sugar lump and set it free. His patience was endless, but now and again he thought it necessary to tickle it with a hazel twig to push the lesson home.

I loved being taken out in the trap and would sit entranced, watching the broad back of the pony as it trotted along, answering to the lightest movement of his capable hands on the reins. One day, I followed my grandfather to the end shed where the pony stood in its stall. 'I wish I could ride Bonny,' I said, sidling up to it and stroking its nose.

His expression did not change as he stirred stale bread, the scrapings from our dinner plates, potato peelings and cabbage stalks into the pig bucket, adding sour milk and a handful of barley to the resultant mixture. 'Bonny's not useter being ridden. What would your ma say if you was to fall off and hurt yarself?'

'I won't fall if you hold on to me.' I went

[9]Maw, short for mawther, means miss or girl and is the feminine equivalent of the more common 'bor', meaning boy.

and stood looking down at the unappetising mess in the bucket, which I knew would set the pigs squealing noisily at the orchard gate as soon as he put in an appearance with the pail in his hand. 'Please, Grandad.'

He did not answer but stomped out with the bucket and fed the pigs. The following day, after he came back from an errand, he drew up as usual outside the shed that housed the trap and unharnessed the pony, but instead of leading him into the stable, he threw a blanket over him. 'Come you on then,' he said, lifting me up and setting me astride its back. 'Let's see what sort o' job you mek on it.'

Oh, how proud I was, sitting up there so far from the ground, as he led me up and down the orchard, keeping a watchful eye on the pony. But he had been right, Bonny was not used to having anyone on his back and he tried to break into a trot, so that Grandad had to run beside him, pulling on the reins, shouting, 'Whoa, boy, Whoa there!'

My pleasure turned to fear as we appeared to be heading straight for the pit. Grandad managed to pull the animal up before we all pitched headlong over the fence that separated the orchard from the steep slope down to the water and then turned us back towards the house. We were met by Uncle Arthur who had no doubt been sent by my grandmother. He took over the reins, grumbling at Grandad for running up and down at his age. 'That's enough for one day,' he said to me, as he led the pony back to the garden gate and he lifted me down. 'D'you want your grandpa to drop dead?'

Worried about what my uncle had said about dropping down dead, I did not dare ask to ride the pony again and though I would not admit it, I had been a little frightened. Grandad would never tolerate anyone's nervousness of animals, though I did hear a story that he had once been chased by a bull and vaulted a five-barred gate like an Olympian athlete.

It always amazed me that whatever job needed doing on the farm, the wherewithal was there to do it. My grandparents seemed to have few material possessions, but they never threw anything away and even gave some things a secondary use, like the old shepherd's hut, and the weed hook, which seemed tailor-made for blackberrying. Scythes, sickles, whetstones, old seed barrows, horse troughs and ancient apple wood ploughs, they were all there, stored in numerous outhouses. There was an old water cart parked against the hedge in the orchard. Its small wheels were rusted and overgrown with nettles and the ubiquitous bindweed, almost as if it had taken root itself. But I saw it moved once.

There had been a long drought, plants were drooping and livestock panting from lack of water; the level in the well had dropped so that Grandad was drawing up little frogs in the bucket, a sure sign it was getting low. The pit, which never dried up completely, was certainly down, tin cans and bottles, once safely submerged began to show themselves and cows got stuck in its muddy edges trying to reach the water. The little pony, used only for pulling the trap, was harnessed to the old water cart, dragged manually from its bed under the hedge. He did not think much of this ignominy and balked at being backed between the lichen-covered wooden shafts.

'Gitcher in there,' Grandad commanded as Bonny frisked his hind legs in protest. 'Yer grut jenny, git you in afore I fetch you one.' He lifted the back of his hand over the pony's nose, in much the same gesture as he used to us when we annoyed him, and it had the same effect. The pony allowed itself to be hitched to the cart and persuaded with a combination of gentleness and threats to pull the contraption down the Drift to the pit. Here another performance took place to make it back the cart down the slope to the water, grown steeper and muddier because of the drought, but it was achieved in the end, the container was filled and taken back to the orchard for the rest of the animals and the garden. Miraculously it did not leak. Although it had taken the best part of the morning, Grandad was triumphant. 'I hatta fare wrassle[10] with him,' he told Grandma. 'But he know who's master in the end.'

There is no doubt my grandfather intended to be master, but he could be gentle with sick animals and their welfare would always come before his own comfort. Vets were rarely called except for horses. It was not that Grandad begrudged the fee, although in the early days that would have taken some finding, but because he was supremely confident of his own ability. He always reckoned he knew as much about his charges as any 'animal doctor' and if he could not see to them, then no one could. People came to ask his advice about sick and pregnant animals in much the same way as humans turned to my grandmother.

He had a great storehouse of remedies in the stable: salves, ointments, powders, scours, sweet nitre, Stockholm tar, turpentine and Jeyes fluid (which he used to treat sheep maggots), linseed oil and turpentine. Sometimes if anyone in the house was unwell, he would say, 'I ha' got just the thing for that in the end shud.' Grandma always said he was 'hevin' us on'[11] and of course he would not dose us like his animals, but we were not too sure and unless we were very ill, ceased to complain for fear of the remedy.

'We're gooin' to cut the top field tomorrow,' he told Grandma towards the end of our holiday.

I pricked up my ears. 'Can we go?'

Grandma smiled. 'I expect so, if you're good.'

At harvest time, neighbouring farmers would pool their manpower, going from farm to farm in turn and the following day it would be the turn of my grandfather.

'One time, the men used to get extra wages for harvest,' Grandma explained, as we all sat down for tea. 'The farmers want it done as soon as the corn was ready and they want it finished in 24 days, so the labourers, for once, hev the upper hand. One man, called the Lord of the Harvest, was picked by the workers to bargain with the master. Sometimes they went at it hammer and tongs for hours, the master wanted it done cheap and the Lord of the Harvest want every penny he kin get, but in the end it were all cut and dried. The Lord usually got £7 or £8 at the end of the harvest and the men about 30 shillings less. They would decide how much corn evraone would be give as a bonus. If we were lucky it would be a coomb, that's four bushels,[12] and glove money too.'

'Glove money?' I queried.

'In times gone by the farmer give his

---

[10]wrestle

[11]teasing

[12]A bushel is a measure of capacity. It is equivalent to 36.4 litres.

men gloves to work in on account of the thistles, but later they just give extra money, it was up to you whether you bought gloves with it. They seal the bargain with a drink, "wetting the scythe", they call it, and then the Lord git his men together and give them their hiring money, which were usually a shilling and then he pick his lady.'

She saw my eyebrows go up in an unspoken question and laughed. 'Not a real lady, just another of the men to be his second in command. In the days afore reapers, the Lord set the pace with his scythe and the men work across the field in a long line keeping to his time.'

Grandad was expert with the scythe. I remember one hanging on the wall in the stable, which he took down and sharpened periodically in order to mow the grass in the orchard. It was wonderful to watch him. He had a very strong, smooth rhythm, turning his body on his sturdy legs to cut the maximum swathe with each stroke, and the heavy scythe would swish through the grass an inch or two above the ground and the long gleaming strands of grass would be laid flat, smelling of all the sweetness of a summer's day.

I cannot smell new-mown grass, even now, without thinking of him and picturing that shining scythe cutting the grass so smoothly and hearing him admonish me. 'Stand clear, maw, or I'll ha' yar legs off.' When I laughed, he would add, 'I mean it. I could tek yar legs off at one swipe. I mind the time when it happened...' Then he would tell me some gory, only half-true tale of someone he knew who had been so disabled. It might have frightened me into standing back, but I never dwelt on it.

One of my brother's earliest memories is of being sent to the harvest field with a message for our grandfather. He has forgotten the message, but he has an enduring memory of seeing him sitting on the ground, with his back to the hedge and his scythe lying beside him, eating his lunch of bread and cheese. He cut a chunk off the bread and put it straight into his mouth off the tip of the knife, and then did the same with the cheese. On the grass beside him was a stone jar containing cider or beer with which he washed it down.

By time I arrived on the scene, the scythe was only used to cut the headland, a width of corn around the circumference of the field sufficient to allow two cart horses pulling the reaper to plod round without trampling down standing corn.

'It's called opening up,' Grandad explained. 'It tek a bit o' time with two on us working side by side. We tie the corn into sheaves with binder twine and stand 'em in the hedge, then the horses brung the reaper in. That time o' day it only cut the corn, it didn't bind it. The cut corn were left on the field for the women and childer to gather up and bind into sheaves, then they stook it.'

'Didn't they go to school?' I asked.

'It were the harvest holiday,' he said sharply. Schooling was a sore subject with him and he was very defensive. 'They larn all they need to know in the fields.'

I liked trudging off to the harvest field in my school holidays to help stook the sheaves that the binder had tied and thrown out behind it. We propped eight together, so that they stood in straight rows across the field like soldiers on parade. Mind you, I did not go until the 'fields were aired' as my grandmother put it, meaning that the sun was well up and everyone else had been hard at work for some time.

Nothing could beat the excitement of seeing a field of wheat cut, especially for a town child. The sun shone from a clear blue sky on to a golden sea, rippling in the heat-haze, dotted with the scarlet of poppies, the purple tufts of giant thistles, not too many of those if the field had been properly cultivated, and the clear blue of cornflowers. Occasionally a pheasant strutted out of the standing corn, holding its head proudly, then it would take off, its wings cracking the air, until it reached the safety of the woods. The little ranny[13] would scamper away on its tiny feet, terrified of the noise of that great lumbering machine coming ever closer to its home. Occasionally a rabbit bolted, but mostly they took refuge in the remaining stand of corn.

Round and round went the harvester, hour after hour, leaving six inches of stubble and an ever diminishing rectangle of standing wheat. The heat and the exertion made everyone hot and sticky. Grandad wore a collarless striped shirt with the sleeves rolled down to protect his arms, but he did not bother to button the cuffs. On his head was a brown trilby, which he doffed every now and again to wipe the back of his arm across his forehead. Others sported big white handkerchiefs tied with a knot at each corner to protect their heads from the sun, but many went bareheaded. The women wore hats and scarves and some of them, even in the 1930s, donned the traditional floppy bonnets of the countrywoman. Children of all ages ran freely about the cut area, but were checked whenever they approached too close to the machinery and its fearsome blades.

Lunch was eaten in the shade of the hedge: bread, slices of beef, chunks of cheese, tomatoes and strong smelling onions, washed down with beer or tea or, for the younger ones, lemonade made with crystals.

By late evening, the rectangle in the middle had shrunk so that only one more circuit by the plodding horses would finish it. Everyone gathered in tense expectation round the perimeter of those last few rows; if hands had been outstretched they would almost have touched. We all had clubs or thick sticks; on some harvest fields men with guns stood by, trigger fingers itching, but we did not have firearms, perhaps because Grandad did not own a gun or perhaps because Grandma always maintained that shot ruined a rabbit for eating.

Bravely I stood, stick in hand, and watched the last whirring of the reaper sails and the cut wheat disappearing and then the shout. 'There they go!' as the rabbits ran out from their last remaining refuge. Oh, how they ran. Hither and thither in a panic they dodged, chased and clubbed by shouting, excited children and cool-headed, determined men. The men linked the dead rabbits' back legs, by opening one leg with a sharp knife and pulling the other paw through the tendon. In that way, they could be threaded on a long stick to be borne home. By the end of the day, there were several sticks of rabbits waiting to be carried from the field. But my soft upbringing came to the fore. I could not kill.

'You duzzy fule! What are you a-doing on?' Grandad demanded, highly annoyed

[13]mouse

because I had allowed a good fat rabbit to run between my legs and escape. I liked rabbit stew, especially when Grandma made it with carrots and onions from the garden and a rich brown gravy, but if I had to kill the animal first, I would rather go without. He was still incensed when he took us home.

'Let her be,' Grandma said. 'She i'n't used to country ways, you can't expect her to do like the village children.'

But my brother had. He had bagged a good adult rabbit and was bearing it from the field in triumph when our uncle and another man came up and took it off him, saying they would 'tek care on it' and he had not dared to protest. So, like me, he was empty-handed, though for a different reason.

A few days after the harvest, the stooks were dismantled and loaded on to wagons and taken to wherever the stack was going to be made, usually in the corner of the field. The base on which the rick was going to be built was carefully constructed to prevent rats getting into the corn and to keep it dry. Balks of timber were laid across stones about two feet high and wider at the top than the bottom so that the rodents could not run up them. Smaller timbers were laid crossways on top and then layered with brushwood and finally straw, so that a good firm floor was made. The stack was built on this, beginning with a sheaf standing right in the middle. Others were laid tightly and neatly round it with the cut ends of the stalks outwards. When the rick was finished the ears of wheat were all safely inside and all you could see were the cut ends of the stalks. Then it was thatched and left until threshing time.

The men worked quickly and meticulously, putting each sheaf down exactly so and being careful not to shake it so the grain was lost, alive to the knowledge that the prosperity of the farm depended on their work and any slackness would be paid for with hunger.

In spite of all the trouble taken to prevent it, rats did get into the corn and ratting was a popular sport with the young lads of the village during the early part of the winter when the nights were drawing in. 'They'd set off two or three together, with lanterns and a dog,' my grandmother explained. 'They shade their lanterns and hold the dog in check while they creep up close to the stack. Then they uncover the light and the rats get caught in the glare and freeze with fright. The dog mek short work on 'em then. Then they lay the corpses nose to tail across the farmer's gateway and he reward 'em with a few coppers.'

Harvest had changed little between the years when Grandad was young and I was a girl. I saw an odd tractor or two, but they had not completely superseded the horses. The machinery had improved, but gaining the harvest was still labour-intensive, still just as physically exhausting. But when my grandfather was young he could look forward to Harvest Horkey, a celebration that had died out by the time I appeared on the scene. It was usually preceded by 'hollerin' largesse', when all the young men who had taken part in the harvest, toured the village with ribbons in their caps, knocking on doors and demanding money. The proceeds were used to finance a party at one of the village pubs, the Three Tuns, the Carpenter's Arms, the Windmill or the Good Woman.

The horkey itself, called a 'frolluck' by my grandparents was paid for by the farmer and was usually held in a big barn that had been cleared to make way for trestle tables loaded with cold cooked beef, ham, cheese and pickles, apple pie and plum duff, with beer to drink. The farmer made a speech thanking his workers and the Lord of the Harvest replied on their behalf. Everyone was happy and relaxed; another harvest had been safely gathered in and now they could enjoy themselves. They ate and drank, danced and sang, and Walter pursued Eliza with a singleness of purpose that convinced her he was serious.

She began to collect bits and pieces for her bottom drawer, linen carefully stitched by hand, patchwork quilts, feathers for stuffing pillows, and rag rugs. She was still making rugs 40 years later. They were made from any material that came to hand: old discarded clothes, stockings, blankets, dressmaker's scraps from her rag bag and from anyone else who could be persuaded to part with them. There was a story attached to each piece of material; this had come from a favourite dress, or this was part of a skirt one of the children had worn, this was a piece of one of Grandad's shirts, that was a satin night-dress, part of someone's trousseau. The cloth was cut into strips about half an inch wide and three or four inches long. These were knotted into a sackcloth backing, making whatever pattern you fancied.

I used to help her sometimes, sitting on the little chair near enough to work on the opposite end of the backing, choosing the colours carefully to make a pattern, pushing the hook through and drawing the doubled material back through the canvas and passing the ends through the loop to make a knot. I tried to keep a straight line, but if I did not, it showed and I am sure Grandma pulled it out and did it again after I had gone to bed, though she never told me she did. We would sit working by the light of the oil lamp while I listened to her tales of bygone days.

'That time o' day, when Grandad was young not all the farmers could afford to buy the new machinery,' she told me. 'It were a long time afore they clubbed together to buy a troshin'[14] machine. They'd take the tackle from farm to farm and if you were walking along the lanes when they come by, you'd have to jump into the hedge out o' their way. It need four horses to pull the ingine and four more to pull the troshin' drum and there'd be two pulling the elevator and one with the chaff cutter and another with the water tank, which they hatta hev to cool the ingine. How many do you mek that?'

'12,' I said triumphantly, after a moment's thought. 'But how did they do the troshing before they had the machines?'

My question had been prompted because earlier that day I had taken my grandfather his packed lunch when he was threshing in the corner of one of the fields. I remember the heat, not only from the sun, which seemed always to be shining in those days, but from the petrol engine; and the noise and the smell, oily and dusty, making breathing difficult. Grandad was covered with a light powdery dust which caked on his lips and made his hair white. It was hardly surprising that he always had a prodigious thirst and my arrival with his bread and cheese, signalled the time to stop

[14]threshing

and slake it from the stone jar, called a 'stoone hoss', kept in the shade somewhere handy.

When they returned to work, I stood and watched as the grain streamed into sacks held open under the body of the machine. It cascaded in with an irregular whoosh like a tap that is momentarily turned off, then on again. The straw was carried up the elevator to the men making the stack, its angle getting steeper and steeper as the stack grew until I thought it would stop and start slipping down again. But it did not and the men on the stack seemed to be working in the sky, arms and backs bending and straightening, legs buried, as they tried to keep up with the remorseless machine. Chaff flew everywhere and stuck on your hair and clothes, even if, like me, you were only a spectator.

'One time, the corn were took into the barn on wagons piled so high you could barely see the wagon,' my grandmother said, stopping to select several pieces of cut material from the basket on the floor at her side and laying them across her knee ready for knotting. 'They were driv' through the big double doors of the barn into the middlestead, that's the space in the middle. Then it was heaped on a platform at one end. They hev to pack it in real tight and sometimes they got a boy on a horse to ride round and round on it, pushing it down and getting higher and higher while the others kept heaping it in. He got up so high it were a job to get the horse down agin and it hatta be helped with ropes thrown over a beam.'

I was not sure if she was telling a tall story, she did that sometimes, but her expression was perfectly serious; but then she could always keep a straight face when she was teasing and you could never be sure.

'Then what?' I asked, forgetting my knotting, though she continued to work.

'They left it there 'til the ploughing was done and the winter wheat was set, then they pulled it out into the middlestead floor and trosh it with flails.'

'What's a flail?'

'Questions, questions, questions,' said Grandad, coming in the back door and hanging his jacket on the hook behind it. He sat down in his chair and groped beneath it for his slippers. 'What's she want to know now?'

'What's a flail?' I repeated.

'A stick an' a half,' he said, smiling at his own little joke. I looked from one to the other while he savoured the moment.

'It's a short stick and a long stick joined together with a bit o' leather.' As usual it was my grandmother who satisfied my curiosity. 'Just like your arm is joined at the elbow, only one is longer than the other and it can bend both ways. You hold the long bit in your hand and whip the heap of corn on the floor with the other end and that make the grain fall out. You work in pairs and you hatta be careful not to fetch each other a clump. The chaff and straw get blown away with a dressing machine and what's left is grain for the miller. If it hev bin a good harvest troshin' go on well into the winter and keep the men at work when they might ha' bin stood off, then they hev a few extra coppers in their pockets.' She always referred to money as coppers, rarely pounds, shillings and pence, unless she wanted to mention a specific figure. 'That was when everyone had new boots.'

'I dessay I ha' got a flail in the shud,' Grandad said. 'I'll show you tomorrow if I happ'n on it.' He paused and looked up at the clock on the mantelpiece. 'Time you were abed.'

'Let me finish this row,' I begged, turning my attention back to the rug.

'Bed,' he repeated, lifting down a candle in a plain enamelled candlestick and lighting it from the fire with a spill taken from a holder beside the clock. 'I'm goin' m'self direc'ly.'

'But its only seven o'clock.' I knew it was useless to argue even though I tried. Dusk was called 'shutting in time' and Grandad had been conditioned to going to bed when it grew dark and getting up as soon as it became light enough to see. That way you made the maximum use of daylight and saved on candles and oil.

'Tomorrow is another day,' Grandma said. 'And John will be fast asleep by now.' My brother, younger by two years, was sent to bed ahead of me, so that we did not spend half the night talking.

So I took my candle and crept up the twisting stair to the big double bed with its deep feather mattress and soft white pillow, made of the best down. I set the candle down on the table beside the bed, undressed quickly, made a pretence of washing and climbed in. I would lie there, almost drowning in down, watching the shadows made by the flickering candle across the uneven ceiling and think about those days long ago, before I had been born. It was easy for me to imagine it because the house, the village and the countryside had hardly changed. I was there with them as I drifted off to sleep.

Courtship and a Wedding

I NEVER STOPPED asking questions because I loved to hear my grandparents talk in their broad, slow dialect, and learn about days gone by. Grandma was the best story teller; she believed in putting a little romance into things, where Grandad was severely practical. She could transport you back in time so completely that, looking back now, it is difficult to separate the things I witnessed myself and the things she merely told me about.

But I do remember being taken gleaning, although when I went the corn we gathered was used for chicken feed and not for grinding into flour; it was not the important source of food it had once been. When we arrived there was already a crowd of women and children on the stubble field, all moving forward more or less in line, picking up stray ears of corn and even spilled grains, putting them into sacks. There was nothing difficult about it, but it was backbreaking and the results of my labour would hardly have fed a mouse.

Gleaning was another of the farm jobs that necessitated absence from school in the days of my grandparents' childhood. 'We couldn't begin until the farmer let us,' Grandma said as we walked home with the small sack of grain balanced on the handlebars of her bicycle. 'We'd all be at the gate

of the field ready to start, but we dussn't set foot inside while the policeman was there.'

'It was guarded by a policeman?' Was this another of her jokes?

'Not a real one,' she explained. 'It were the name we give to the last stook of corn left in the field after all the others ha' bin took off. You couldn't glean while it was there, but the minute someone from the farm come to fetch it away, we all rush in.'

'Why was it left there?'

'So's to be fair, dew[15] those that lived nearest would get in first and get a head start.'

'What did you do with the corn you picked up? Did you give it to the farmer?'

'That we didn't. We keep what we gleaned, it was part of the harvest bargain. We took it to the miller's and had it ground into flour for making bread.'

'You won't make bread with this, though,' I said, holding the garden gate open while she pushed her bicycle through and up to the shed.

'No, it's not worth the grinding, but it'll do for the hens.'

'Did you bake bread?' I asked as we stood the sack of corn in the corner of the end shed and made our way back into the house.

[15]or, otherwise

'Almost everyone did then. Now, of course, if we want to bake bread, we buy the flour from the grocer and the yeast from the baker. I'll make some for you tomorrow, if you like.'

And so she did, using the oven of the kitchen range, though there was a little cupboard beside it that she told me had once been a bread oven. Now she kept her letter writing materials, pencils, a steel-nibbed pen and a bottle of Quink in it.

'We used whin faggots to heat it,' she said.

'Gorse,' I said, remembering her tales of the brick kiln.

'Yes, we put the faggots directly into the oven and set light to 'em. The oven wasn't hot enough until they burned out and the bricks turn from black to red. While it was getting hot, we mixed the dough with yeast saved from the last brew of beer and set it to prove in a bowl with a cloth over it. When the dough had riz we mek it into loaves and leave it a little longer while we scrape all the ash out, then we set the loaves direc'ly on the floor of the oven and shut the door right quick to keep the heat in. You know they're done if they sound hollow when you tap the bottom. Afterwards, if the oven was still hot, you might bake other things in it, a cake or a stew that you could leave in there a long time while the oven cool.'

Although she did not bake her own bread regularly any more, the little loaves, still warm from the oven and spread with butter, tasted delicious.

'Grandad's mother didn't like the bread that were baked by the miller in the village,' Grandma told me. 'She want the bread that come from Swaffham. It was delivered by horse and cart, but the bread-man wouldn't come down the Drift for the sake of one loaf, so he leave it with Mrs Powley and she fetch it from there.'

Mrs Powley's daughter, Dolly, a younger sister of the three who had gone through the ice, remembers Walter's mother walking up the Drift to collect the bread. 'She wore black lace-up boots, a long black skirt and a black cape held with a chain at the neck,' she told me. 'Her hat was like a big black pancake and she kept it on with a hat pin.'

Hilda Saunders, daughter of Vi Fickling, another of my grandmother's lifelong friends, who lived up near the chapel when she was a child told me of the day the baker's horse bolted at the end of Chapel Lane. 'It didn't make the bend into Leather Bottle Lane and went into the river, horse, cart, the lot,' she said. 'All the bread was floating about on the water. My father and uncle went to help fetch the horse and cart out.'

While this was going on more than a few of the loaves found themselves being dried off in ovens around Ivy Todd. That happened in the 1920s, in the middle of the depression, and would have seemed like manna from heaven. But I am getting ahead of myself. Grandma was telling me about her courtship as the 19th century turned into the 20th.

Though the turn of the century was celebrated with optimism as the start of a new era and perhaps better times, it was short-lived; the summer of 1900 saw hailstones as big as walnuts flatten the growing crops. One, which crashed through a bedroom window of one cottage, was recorded as being eight inches in circumference. Once again the farmers were living from hand to mouth.

'We couldn't afford to get married,' she told me. 'Grandad was still helping out at home and if he married, his parents would miss the money he brung in. We had nowhere to live. We hatta wait until a tied cottage come empty.'

'What's tied mean?'

'It mean the house belong to the farmer and goes with the job. Most workers in those days live in tied houses. If you left your job or were let go, then you hatta get out of the house.'

They had been 'walking out' for five years; Walter's sister, Hannah, had become Mrs Arthur Akers and Elizabeth had become Mrs Alfred Hicks. Eliza's 21st birthday, both the pretended one and the real one, came and went and they seemed no nearer to being married.

'Mind you, we weren't down in the mouth, nor working the hull time,' she said. 'We hev our amusements too, though we didn't have much money to spend on them. There was donkey racing in the market at Swaffham and sometimes there were theatricals in the yard of the Oak and we'd pay tuppence to go in.'

Swaffham was the centre of most of the leisure activity in the neighbourhood and it was there they repaired in search of entertainment and diversion, besides shopping for those things that could not be obtained in the village stores. Walter and Eliza, on rare days off, joined in whatever was going on and visited Eliza's grandparents, who had moved there from Necton. Whether she went to see her father and two sisters, I do not know. I know she missed Alice, who was now working in Hunstanton. It

was still a good few miles distant but at least it was in the same county, and they could still write to each other.

They also went to the fairs held in May, July and November, which were mainly for the sale of cattle and sheep, but also included amusements and entertainment. It was also where the hiring fairs were held. With farming so badly in the doldrums, workers were taken on only for as long as the farmer thought he could pay them. If things went well he extended their contract for another year, otherwise the labourers resorted to standing in the market place on hiring days and tried to appear skilled, experienced and enthusiastic as potential employers looked them over. They would wear or carry something denoting their trade: the horseman carried a horse brass or a whip, the shepherd his crook, the housemaid a bucket and scrubbing brush, the milkmaid her three-legged stool.

'We need a house to live in,' Grandma said. 'Grandad had bin promised the next one to come along, so he hatta stay where he was, though it mean waiting for someone to move on or die.'

In January of the following year, Queen Victoria died and plunged the whole country into mourning. Black was the colour of the day. Clothes were black, cards were edged in black, furniture was draped in black, at least among the upper classes; the workers had no money for such niceties. The dumpy little queen, who had dressed in heavy mourning ever since Prince Albert's death, 40 years before, had made the monarchy popular. She had been the great matriarch of Europe; her children and grandchildren were scattered among the royal houses of Germany, Russia, Romania, Sweden and Norway.

I remember Grandma giving me a large gold covered book to look at, which listed the hierarchy of the royal family in great detail and had a wealth of pictures and photographs. Where or how Grandma had acquired it, I do not know. It was the genealogy that fascinated me; who was related to whom and how the whole great dynasty had spread far and wide. I likened it to our own family, begun in my mind with the Brown and Ong great-grandparents whose children were scattered over the country, each starting their own little section of the family.

The new King's coronation, fixed for August the following year, had to be delayed because he needed an appendix operation. There was much argument in the village as to whether the celebrations should be cancelled. 'Some say the King were ill and we oughta be praying for his recovery instead,' Grandma told me. 'But most of the food had already been bought and it would be squinged[16] if we didn't use it, so we went ahead, but the children didn't get their mugs until the proper Coronation Day.'

Eliza and Walter, who was 30 and still living with his parents, seemed no nearer getting married and were beginning to wonder how much longer they would have to wait. Sometimes their impatience got the better of them and in the summer of 1903, Eliza realised she was pregnant.

Fifty or so years before, over 25 per cent of women were pregnant when they married, 'cuckolding the parson' they used to call it. Indeed, in many rural communities the practice was actively encouraged.

Labourers needed to know that the girls their sons married were capable of producing children, not, as in the case of the upper classes, in order to inherit wealth and titles, but so that they would have someone to look after them in their old age. The alternative was the workhouse and the spectre of that was dreaded well into this century. I often heard my grandparents speak of it as something to be avoided at all costs.

It was the middle class Victorians who, on the surface at least, condemned sex outside marriage and this attitude filtered down to the lower orders, especially to those aspiring to better themselves like David and Sarah Ong, who had no cause to censure the young couple. Their son, Charles, had been born the day after their wedding.

Eliza must have been at her wits' end, not knowing where to turn for help. Her mother was dead and her Brown grandparents had moved to Swaffham and, in any case, were now quite elderly, and she could hardly confide in any of her uncles. Walter was supportive and probably worried to death, but there was no sympathy to come from his parents. His mother blamed Eliza for leading her son astray. I think Walter must have had quite an unpleasant time of it at home then.

I do not know if Mrs Benstead knew about the pregnancy or whether Eliza managed, with tight corseting and full skirts, to keep the truth hidden. She was worried about keeping her job at the Three Tuns, which was vital until such time as she and Walter could afford to marry, not only because of the money but because it was also her home. Luck was a little on her side because she had arranged to spend

[16]spoiled, go rotten

Christmas in Fakenham with her Aunt Sarah, who had three small sons of her own. Alfred was born there on Christmas Eve 1903. The day after Boxing Day, Eliza left her two-day-old son with her aunt and cousins and went back to Necton and her job.

Eliza and Walter about the time of their marriage, 1904.

My grandmother did not tell me this. At the time I was quizzing her, I was a small child and such things were not for a little girl's ears, but she did tell my cousin, Joan, Alfred's daughter, many years later when she was grown up and married and expecting her first child.

'He came a bit earlier than we expected,' she told her. 'I didn't know he was coming until he was nearly here.' I do not think she meant she did not know the facts of life; she was after all a countrywoman and she had been present when her youngest sister had been born, but simply that he arrived a little prematurely. 'And I didn't have a crib

The interior of All Saints' Church. The church is noted for its medieval roof, which was added on to the earlier building in the late 15th century and restored in 1982.

for him, so we put him on a pillow in a drawer.' Joan was staying at Necton at the time she was being told this story, and Grandma fetched out a tissue wrapped package, which she reverently put into her hands. 'This is the pillow case he was laid on. I want you to have it.' She was never tearful, but I think she might have been very close to it on that occasion. I know Joan was very moved.

Sarah Ong bowed to the inevitable after this and accepted that Walter and Eliza would marry. When, in the spring, a cottage became available at Ivy Todd Farm and was offered to Walter, they put plans in hand for a wedding. But before that could take place, another blow was to fall. Grandfather Brown died in May and there was a funeral to attend. Eliza was very sad at the loss of her grandfather. He had been a hard taskmaster, but a fair one. He, like her grandmother, had never been judgmental.

So it was not on her grandfather's arm she went to All Saints' Church, Necton on 30 July 1904, nor her father's, but her Uncle Harry's. She dressed in her best frock and carried a posy of flowers plucked from the garden. It was not a grand affair and the guests were few. Grandmother Brown was there, but the fact that it was her Uncle Harry who gave her away suggests that her father did not put in an appearance. Whether any of her sisters came I do not know. Her Aunt Sarah were there, supportive as always, and her Uncle Benjamin, Walter's best man, who had married a local girl and still lived in Necton. Walter's parents were there and his sister, Florence.

Grandma told me of the events of that day with a chuckle as if the whole thing was a great joke and I don't suppose it was the first time, or the last, when her sense of humour came to her rescue.

The service went smoothly enough, though there were no church bells, nor choir. Sarah Ong did not think such things were appropriate given the circumstances.

Certificate of Marriage.

1904	Marriage Solemnized at the parish Church in the parish of Necton in the County of Norfolk.							
No.	When Married.	NAME AND SURNAME.	Age.	Condition.	Rank or Profession.	Residence at the Time of Marriage.	FATHER'S NAME AND SURNAME.	Rank or Profession of Father.
351	July 30 1904	Walter Ong	30	Bachelor	Labourer	Necton	David Ong	Farmer
		Eliza Marie Brown	24	Spinster	—	Necton	John Brown	Brickmaker

Married in the parish Church of Necton according to the Rites and Ceremonies of the Established Church after Banns
By me, Thos. Phillips, Curate, Necton

This Marriage was solemnized between us, {Walter Ong / Eliza Marie Brown} In the presence of us, {Harry Brown / Florence Ong}

The above is a true Copy of the Marriage Register of the parish Church of Necton aforesaid, the said Register being legally in my custody.
Extracted this thirtieth day of July in the Year of our Lord
By me, Thos. Phillips Curate of Necton
One Thousand Nine Hundred and four.

Walter and Eliza's marriage certificate. Eliza was in fact 22, and Walter 32. Note also that Walter and Eliza did not sign the certificate themselves.

Afterwards the bride and groom left the congregation in the church porch and set off to walk the three miles to the little cottage at Ivy Todd Farm, where they were to make their home.

'We got as far as Grummet's shop, when a fair owd tempest blew up and it start to rain cats and dogs,' she said, eyes twinkling at the memory. 'We were fare soaked in no time. We sheltered in the doorway of the shop and then Mrs Grummet come out and took pity on us. She invite us in and give us a cup of tea, but it was the middle of the summer and she didn't have a fire going, so we couldn't get dry. Howsummever, when the rain let up, we set out again.

'I was shivering and Grandad happen to have a half bottle of whisky in his pocket that Ben give him for a wedding present, so

Billy Green at the crossroads in the tiny hamlet of Ivy Todd (population about 30). The Carpenter's Arms on the corner closed as a pub in 1955. The stream is a tributary of the River Wissey. Eliza and Walter's first home once stood just behind the pub. Photo courtesy of Eastern Counties Newspapers Ltd.

he took it out and offered it to me. I weren't goin' to say no, cos me teeth were chattering. Besides, it was our wedding day. He'd just got the top off and was handing it to me when up come a pony and trap. It was Grandad's father and mother. They'd been sheltering in the church porch and weren't wet at all. They pulled up

'longside us and the old lady reached out and snatched the bottle out o' Grandad's hand. She give us a talking to about the evils of strong drink, then she turn to Grandad Ong and bid him drive on.'

David Ong flicked the reins and the pony started off again, leaving the newly-wed pair in the middle of the road, still soaking wet and without the means for even a small celebration. This was perhaps a strange attitude for an ex-publican to take, although the Jolly Farmers had only sold beer and not spirits, and besides, the Ongs had bettered their standing in the community and they meant to live up to it. Or at least, Sarah did. David Ong, according to my grandmother was not nearly so fierce and uncompromising as his wife.

'What happened to the bottle of whisky?' I asked.

Grandma shrugged. 'I don't know. We never saw it again.'

Walter and Eliza had very little in the way of possessions with which to furnish their cottage, but it was so tiny little was needed. Some bits and pieces they bought in Swaffham market and had them delivered by the carrier's cart. They had been given a few things by relatives and with Eliza's bottom drawer of linen and rag rugs, they managed well enough.

One of my grandmother's most prized possessions, and it remained so throughout her long life, was a blue-patterned bone china tea set – a dozen plates, cups and saucers, a teapot, milk jug and slop basin, given to her as wedding present by her beloved Grandmother Brown. It must have been old then; something from her own china cabinet. It was never hidden away unused, but came out on every family occasion or when anyone came to call and was offered a cup of tea. Everyone except Grandma was terrified of breaking it, but she always maintained it was meant to be used. She even lent it to other people; it was well known in the village at weddings and funeral teas and even at Women's Institute functions. The Ellis family borrowed it in 1925 when Mr Ellis was buried, and one cup was broken, and it was on loan to a local organisation for a tea party in the village hall as late as 1960, when two more pieces were smashed. Grandma took the disasters philosophically and shrugged her shoulders when we told her on that last occasion that she was mad to let it out of the house. 'It's like its owner,' she said. 'It's had a good innings.'

They were happy in their new home and Eliza made a good, affectionate and hard-working wife. As soon as they could, they went to Fakenham and fetched baby Alfred home. How his sudden arrival was greeted in the village, we do not know. It was a close-knit community where everyone knew everyone else's business, or thought they did, and there must have been a few raised eyebrows and whispering behind their backs. But Eliza was very gutsy and she would not have been intimidated by them; she would have held her head up. I know she eventually earned the respect of everyone including her parents-in-law.

'Grandad's wages went up to 10 shillings a week,' my grandmother told me, while I followed her round the house and garden hanging on her every word. 'He was a proper shepherd by then, o' course, and his animals always hatta come first. I used to say he were wedded to them there sheep. He'd be out in all weathers, even when there was snow up to your armpits. He used to make himself snow shoes to get across the land. At lambing time I hardly saw anything of him. He slept in a little shepherd's hut on wheels out in the pasture alonga the sheep, until all the ewes had safely lambed. It had a little stove in it for heating water to make a cup of tea and warm some dinner. He'd warm milk for orphan lambs too.

'Many's the time he's brung me in a baby lamb to look after. In a hard winter, the ewes sometimes don't make enough milk and their lambs hatta be hand reared. I used to feed them from a medicine bottle with a teat on it 'til they were weaned or 'til Grandad could persuade another ewe to take them. Ewes don't take kindly to fostering orphan lambs, you know. If a ewe lost her lamb to a fox, Grandad would wipe the fleece over the orphan and shut the two on 'em in together. That usually do the trick.'

Shepherding was a skilled and responsible job and the shepherd enjoyed a freedom and independence denied the ordinary farm worker. From the time the lambs were born, often in the depths of winter, until they went off to market, the shepherd was responsible for their well-being and took a great pride in his job. The young lambs had to be weaned and their tails docked. The ram lambs, except those selected for breeding, had to be castrated and you could not be squeamish if you had that job to do.

'He hatta dock the lambs' tails,' she said. 'He burn them off with a hot iron, then he'd skin the tails and bring 'em home alonga the sweetbreads, for me to make a stew.' When I screwed up my face in distaste, she smiled. 'You may turn your nose up, my girl, but it was good and nourishing, especially when you couldn't afford to buy meat from the butcher.'

The shepherd received half a coomb of malt at lambing time and 'lambing money', a bonus for every healthy lamb born, but he often had to wait for the lambing sales before it was put into his hand. Whenever a sheep was killed he was given the 'hid and pluck', in other words, the head and liver, which he took home to help feed the family.

Although Walter knew each of his flock by sight, they still had to be marked, usually by branding, and later sheared. Shearing was a heavy job and required stamina as well as skill, but he had help for that from itinerant shearers who contracted to shear whole flocks. 'They'd cut your hair in their spare time,' Grandma told me. 'They were hully handy with them there shears. Afterwards, there was a feast to celebrate.'

When the sheep had grown their first thickness of new wool, they had to be dipped and as autumn approached the rams were raddled before being put with the ewes for mating. It was a way of colour-coding so that the shepherd could keep track of which of the ewes had been served and when, so that he knew within a few days when to expect the lambs. And when that time came he had to act midwife to the flock and stay with them night and day, hence the hut in the pasture.

'There is a saying,' said my grandmother, who was full of sayings: 'that you trosh wheat to pay the rent, sell some cattle to pay the tithe and the sheep's wool to pay the shepherd. What's left you kin use to pay yourself and your men. The shepherd was a very important man, you know.'

'What's tithe?' I asked.

'It means a tenth. In the old day's you had to pay a tenth of everything you produced to the parson. A tenth of your crops, one in ten of your sheep or cattle...'

'Why?'

She never seemed to tire of my questions and smiled a little as she answered. 'That's how the parson got his living. Later you hatta give him money instead of goods, but it amount to the same thing.'

'We were hard up,' Grandma went on, with masterly understatement, 'but we were happy in our way. When winter was done and it forgive,[17] the snowdrops started to bloom, the wind got warmer and the lambs began to frisk about in the fields, you knew you'd soon be busy again.'

She was talking to me in the orchard, gazing out across the pit with its half dozen tame ducks, to the land the other side. Fleecy clouds drifted across a blue sky and in the distance a horse pulled a plough across a field whose furrows, in long straight lines, looked like an enormous piece of corduroy. 'The land won't wait, you know,' she said. 'When the soil's right and the weather's right, you hatta get on to it.'

'How do you know when it's right?'

She came out of her apparent reverie and turned towards the chicken house, which was really Grandad's old shepherd's van, still being put to use after all those years. I followed as the hens clucked round her, for they knew the bowl she carried held their corn. 'Oh, the farmers can tell,' she said. 'They go on to the fields and pick up a handful of mould and rub it atween their fingers and they can tell.' She smiled suddenly. 'If they still weren't sure, they'd drop their britches and sit on the ground.'

'With bare bottoms?' I asked, deliciously shocked, as I helped her scatter the corn, laughing as the birds fought over it.

'Yes. If it felt warm they knew it was right to set seed, though lots of farmers would only set seed when the moon was waxing; it was supposed to be unlucky any other time.'

'At night?'

'No, course not. You hatta see what you're a-doin'. They used a dibber when they planted beans and suchlike. It was a bit like a garden fork, only instead of prongs it had two wooden stumps for making holes in the ground. Grandad would walk across the field pushing it into the ground on his right when his left foot was forward and to the left when his right foot was in front. That way the holes were evenly spaced. A maid go next putting in the seed, four in each hole and a young lad follow behind with a hoe, coverin' on 'em up. He push the earth forward with one chop and level it off with a chop back agin. They go along in a line, holes, seeds, chop, chop, the hull day long and they sing a sowing song, leastways, the children did.' She looked up at the clouds as if to bring the verse to mind.

> Four seeds in a hole,
> One for the rook
> And one for the crow,
> One to rot and one to grow.

I liked that and repeated it several times to commit it to memory.

'Corn and turnip seeds were too tiny to have separate holes,' she went on, while the hens crowded round her. 'They were broadcast. When Grandad help his pa, he'd

---

[17] thawed

put a bag of seed round his neck so it lay in on his chest and he'd take a pinch with each finger and thumb and scatter it on both sides as he walked. It hatta be done careful, the right amount, the right length of stride, so it was done even. When the seed sprouted you could see the missed bits and then he'd be in trouble. Every time he pass the field while it was growing the bare patches shew up and Grandad got another squaring up and never hear the last on it. On the more modern farms horses pulled seed barrows and later there were proper drills and no one set seed like that any more.'

'Grandad must have done a lot of walking,' I said, going with her to the nesting boxes to look for eggs. If there were not any there, we would find them under the hedge alongside the orchard; it was as if the hens were hiding them on purpose so we should not take them. Sometimes they laid their eggs in the tall nettles and then we missed them and what a delight it was when a little later, half a dozen fluffy chicks made their appearance behind the hen.

'We walked everywhere, not only up and down the fields, but to school, to church, to market, everywhere.'

'Shanks' pony,' I said, remembering my grandfather using the expression.

'Yes, or hobnail express. There used to be a law that if you walked more'n three miles of a Sunday, you could have a drink at a pub, even if it were the middle of the afternoon. Grandad and Mr Powley and my Uncle Ben were great pals time they were boys and they'd walk four or five miles jes' for the pleasure of drinking after hours. They'd be met by the local lads and there might be a scrap atween 'em, but then

Walter rounding up ducklings, watched by Eliza with her grandson, Philip, and Norah.

they'd git together and hev a rare owd time. Sometimes they'd go as far as King's Lynn on the train, jes' for the fun of walking back.'

'Didn't they get tired?' I asked. The two-mile walk from Ivy Todd to the village post office was almost more than I was prepared to take, unless bribed with a halfpenny for sweets. I did not count the miles I roamed about the fields and hedgerows during the course of the day, of course.

'They were used to it,' she said, as we took our eggs through the orchard gate, snecking it carefully behind us. 'Life was a lot simpler then. Cars, aeroplanes, harvesters, the Great War were all in the future. As long as we had enough to eat, that's all that worrited us.'

But if you pressed her, she would declare firmly that she would not want to go back to those times. 'That time o' day, there was no dole,' she said. 'Only parish relief and no one want that if they kin manage without. There was no sick pay, nor pensions to speak of and wages were so low the men couldn't manage unless their women worked too. They used to go cleaning, or did sewing or took in washing. I used to do the laundry for the Three Tuns. I fetched it on Alfred's pram and took it back washed and ironed the next day.'

On the 24 April 1905, nine months after my grandparents' wedding, my mother, Doris Alice was born. It was a difficult birth, accomplished with only the minimum of unskilled help, and the little girl was pulled out feet first. She was born with a dislocated hip, though that was not diagnosed until long after she was grown up and married and X-rays commonplace.

Bringing up a Family

THE RECESSION in farming continued without respite and took its toll of the little family who sometimes had barely enough to eat. Alfred was sturdy enough, full of mischief and always on the go, but Doris was very frail and when illness found its way into the house, she had not the strength to resist it. Eliza nursed her night and day as she grew weaker and weaker.

'It's no good,' she told Walter after yet another anxious night. 'We'll hatta get the doctor. We'll lose her if we don't, she won't go through another night.'

'Who's to pay for that?' Walter demanded, but he was clearly very distressed.

'We'll worry about that later,' his wife told him firmly. 'I'm goin' up to the village.'

There were no telephones, so requests for the doctor to call were left at the post office. He would ride from Swaffham to Necton on horseback and pick up the list from there.

'I'll go. You stay here with Doris.' Walter went off to leave the message before going to work on the farm.

A little later his mother came to see

Necton post office at the turn of the century.

what she could do to help and she was still there when the doctor reined in at the gate. Eliza hurried down the path to meet him.

He did not dismount. 'Bring the child out to me,' he commanded.

'But she's too ill to move.'

'Nonsense, if you want me to see her, you must bring her to me.'

Eliza went back indoors. 'He won't come into the house,' she told her mother-in-law.

They both went to the crib and looked down at the tiny mite who was barely alive. Eliza put out her hands, but hesitated to pick her up. 'She was so fragile, I thought her head or her arms would drop off,' she said. 'So we take two corners of the bottom sheet each and lift her on that to carry her to the gate.'

'Hold her up higher,' commanded the doctor, and they raised the little bundle awkwardly. He poked Doris delicately with his crop, hardly stooping to do so, before saying, 'Take her indoors and come back for your instructions.'

Eliza quietly obeyed but inside she was seething at this harsh treatment. The doctor was a coward and afraid for his own skin and she wished she had never called him. But he was Doris's only hope and so she bit her tongue and returned to the gate to be told what she already knew.

'Your child has scarlet fever. You must keep her quiet and away from everyone. Wring a sheet out in disinfectant and hang it over the door and don't let anyone in 'til it's all over.' She knew he meant until Doris had died, and that made her seethe all the more as he went on, 'Leave messages at the gate for the dairyman and the baker and don't go out yourself. We don't want the contagion spreading.'

'That time o' day, everyone was afraid of the fever,' Grandma explained. 'Lots of children died from it and adults too. Doris was ill for weeks and there were times we almost lost hope.'

'Didn't the doctor ever come into the house?' I asked, horrified at his callousness.

'Not that time. He came in when she had rheumatic fever real bad, but that was later.'

Slowly, day by day, the little one grew stronger and at last the quarantine was lifted and the telltale sheet came down from the door. Life resumed its normal pattern. When Doris learned to walk, much later than most children, she had a slight limp, but no one questioned the reason; she was lucky to be alive and that was something to be thankful for.

Many children under similar circumstances did not survive, which was hardly surprising, given the ignorance and sheer poverty that was rife, and the lack of good nursing. That was the trouble, Eliza decided, most of the village women were too poor to afford skilled help and were so concerned with the daily grind of looking after the healthy ones whose labour earned the bread for the family that they had no time to be good nurses, even supposing they had the vocation. Eliza cared deeply about such things, but at that time was in no position to do anything about it.

The spring of 1907 was unseasonably warm and the temperature on Easter Day reached 73°F, which Eliza, being well on in her third pregnancy, found very uncomfortable. On 26 May, a month after Doris's second birthday, Gladys Audrey was born. With three very small children to look after and the agricultural economy showing no signs of improving, in spite of the Liberal Party landslide in the election the year before, it was a constant battle to make ends meet. Eliza could do little to help except clean the house, sew and cook whatever food was available.

'We grew most on it ourselves,' she told me, wetting her finger to test the flat iron she had just taken from the top of the stove and listening to it sizzle. 'We had vegetables a-plenty in the garden and eggs from the hins and sometimes we had chicken for dinner when one stop laying.' Grandma could make one chicken feed an army, as well I knew; hot the first day, cold the second and the bones boiled up for soup on the third. Nothing was ever wasted. Even the downy feathers were saved to stuff pillows.

'We made butter and cheese with milk from Grandad's father's cows,' she went on. She had an old folded blanket spread on the kitchen table as an ironing cloth and the neatly dampened and rolled linen in a pile beside it. Working with two heavy flat irons alternately, one heating on the stove and one in use, she ploughed her way through it, chatting to me as she did so.

'We brewed our own beer – in March for haysel and harvest and in October for Christmas. We didn't need to shop for much except tea, which was a luxury, sugar, clothes and pots and pans. The time for buying such things was just after harvest when we got paid in a lump. Even then, we didn't need to leave the village; the shop men came to us.

'They'd bring a horse and cart into the yard of the Good Woman, loaded with boots and shoes, trousers, coats and hats, night-shirts, petticoats and bolts of cloth, anything you could think of. They knew the men would be in there spending their harvest pay, and they'd be in a good mood and not so careful of their coppers as their wives. The salesman would say he'd got some wunnerful stock and everything a bargain and the men would hold out their tankards and offer the man a sip before starting to bargain.'

'Did they take it?' I asked, wrinkling my nose at the idea of drinking out of someone else's mug.

'Oh, yes, they knew there'd be no business done if they didn't. Howsumever, the men made sure the mugs were all but empty, so the trader had to refill them; he couldn't hand back an empty tankard. After that, the men would go out to the yard and see what was in the cart. Some of 'em would send for their wives to come and take a look, or they tell the man to take such and such to their homes.'

She handed me a pile of handkerchiefs to damp and fold while she went on. 'We had new boots then, and sometimes top coats and Grandad might have a pair o' new cords and a Sunday neckerchief. I'd buy cambric and linen and calico to make shirts and underwear and, if I could afford it, pretty ribbons to trim it with. Course I didn't have a sewing machine, I stitched it all by hand. Doris and Gladys were both christened together in 1907 and I made their christening robes.'

I had seen some of my grandmother's sewing and marvelled at it. How she managed to make such tiny, almost invisible stitches by the light of candle and oil lamp, I could never fathom, yet she did not wear glasses until quite late in life. There was smocking and herringbone stitch, narrow

Necton school. Photo courtesy of Eastern Counties Newspapers Ltd.

pin-tucking and fine drawn-thread work on tablecloths and pillowcases, patchwork quilts and feather-filled cushions representing hours and hours of close work. It was my grandmother who taught me to darn a sock properly, though I never came to like the task.

Shortly after Gladys's birth, Walter changed his job and started work for Mr Adcock of Chapel Farm. There was a tied cottage in Black Drift opposite David Ong's smallholding that had recently become vacant and went with the job, and this may have been his reason for the move. It was detached and had three bedrooms and a decent sized garden, and being so close to his father's holding it made it easier for Walter to help there in his spare time. Whether Eliza saw that as a blessing or a curse, she never said.

Arthur Charles was born on 12 January 1909 and the family rejoiced at the arrival of a second boy. Although Gladys was not yet two, Eliza coped as she always did and life continued in its usual routines of work and sleep, mixed with little diversions and amusements and occasional tragedies.

After harvest that year the time came for Alfred to start school and by this time there were no two ways about it, school was a must. He was a bright, cheerful, child and went off happily enough, joining up with other children at the top of the Drift and dawdling along the country road to the village school, which his father should have attended, but had not.

It had two rooms, one in which the head teacher taught the top class and another, larger one that could be divided by a folding partition into two separate classrooms. It had a big, pot-bellied stove at one end, which meant that those pupils at the other end were always cold in winter, although they were spared the steam and smell of wet clothes being hung round the stove to dry. There were six standards and the pupils worked their way up, according to their ability, to the top of the sixth standard regardless of age. They were then allowed to leave, provided the school governors were satisfied that they had reached the required proficiency.

Alfred came back on that first day full of tales of school and Doris listened in rapture. The next morning, as soon as her brother had disappeared up the Drift, she squeezed herself through the narrow space under the garden gate and followed him. There was a certain amount of consternation when the teacher of the youngest children discovered she had an extra pupil, a small, bright-eyed four-year-old who refused to go home.

One of the bigger children was despatched to tell Mrs Ong where her daughter was and the classes continued. My mother could not remember whether Eliza went to the school or the headmaster went to her home, but the outcome was that Doris was allowed to join the class and went to school regularly from then on. Truancy was still something of a problem, but Mother was never any trouble and loved school, even when she worked her way to the top class and was taught by the fearsome Mr Stead, the headmaster.

'He was very strict,' she told me. 'Bald as a coot, except for three little hairs on the top of his head, which rose up on end if he was angry. If we saw those hairs rise, we knew we were for it. We'd nudge each other and say, "Look out, old Stead's hair's on end, something's up."'

The girls went to school in black button boots, black stockings and starched aprons over dresses almost to their ankles. The aprons had white goffered frills on the shoulders and Eliza took great pride in sending Doris, and later her sisters, to school starched and spotless.

They took their lunch with them. Bread and butter or bread and jam, but never both butter and jam on the same slice of bread; that was an extravagance denied them. According to my grandfather, even in more affluent times it was still an unnecessary luxury.

There were little compensations though. Each day they passed Grummet's shop on the way to and from school and very occasionally they had a farthing to spend on sweets, but the peak of happiness was the day Mrs Grummet's treacle barrel was emptied. Treacle in those days was sold in bulk and the housewives would take a container to the shop and have the treacle ladled into it. The day nothing more could be got out of the barrel, Mrs Grummet would leave it standing outside the shop when school came out, so that passing children could run their fingers round inside it and suck the sweetness from them. On such occasions they buzzed around it like a swarm of bees. Needless to say, Mrs Grummet was a very popular person with the children, though she was not that particular over hygiene. 'She use the same knife to cut cheese as she did the soap, which come in a long block and she hack off whatever you asked for,' Grandma said.

The children gave long rehearsed concerts at the school, trained by their teachers in little plays like Cinderella, which the young actors enjoyed as much as the audience of parents and relatives. The school was also the venue for lantern slide lectures, usually of a religious nature in aid of some missionary or other, and jumble sales, the proceeds of which went to buy new hymn books. Occasionally, dances were also held in the big room with the partitions folded back.

Sunday was always kept as a special day, although the animals were looked after as usual. 'Farm work hatta go on whatever the day,' my grandmother said. 'Animals don't know it's Sunday, they still want their feed. That's why shepherds and horsemen earned a shilling or so more than the ordinary farm workers who didn't have to work on a Sunday. Milk went sour if you didn't get it to the dairy, but we never made butter on a Sunday, we always used

to say it wouldn't 'come' if we churn on the Sabbath.' She laughed. 'Though there's some say, "The better the day, the better the deed."'

The children did not go out to play on Sunday, nor were they allowed to sew or knit. They could read their bibles or uplifting books or stick pictures into their scrap albums, but that was all. If anyone bought a Sunday paper they were supposed to refrain from reading it until Monday, but I doubt if that rule was strictly observed.

Dolly Bell told me her mother went into Swaffham one Saturday and bought some red and white wool, which her father was going to knit into a scarf for her. 'He started straight away,' she told me. 'But he didn't get it finished by Saturday night and I had set my heart on wearing it for school on Monday, so just to please me he finished it on Sunday. My sister had been going to the Christian Endeavour meetings, held by a Mr Hill at the chapel every year, and she'd got very religious and she was furious when she heard me tell my friends my father had knitted my scarf on a Sunday. According to her I'd shown her up.'

Sarah Ong was not so devout that she would not cook on a Sunday. She made a batch of shortcakes every Sunday morning, ready for tea. This sweet curranty pastry is a family tradition; my mother's shortcakes were delicious, my grandmother's were even better. I never tasted my great-grandmother's, but I am assured they were the best of all. 'We used to go over to see her when we knew she'd be taking them from the oven,' my mother told me. 'They were worth braving my grandmother's sharp tongue for.'

On Sundays the children attended

Sunday school outing, 1912. Doris is in the back row, third from the right. Alfred is seated second from left with Gladys behind him to his left.

Sunday school at the Baptist chapel. They had to have a specified number of attendances in a year to qualify for the annual Sunday school treat and they always made sure they notched up the required amount as the date drew near. For weeks beforehand everyone was on their best behaviour, lest the threat, 'You shan't go to the treat,' be carried out in earnest.

Everyone was dressed in their best on the great day; the girls in clean starched aprons with the frill sticking out stiffly from their shoulders and the boys with collars stiff enough to ensure they kept their heads up; they hurt their chins if they did not. Their boots shone with all the spit and polish that had gone into them the day before.

Sometimes the party was held in the field near the chapel and was always preceded by a short service, which had the best turnout of the whole year. Then there would be a Punch and Judy or a conjuror, followed by a tea of jam or paste sandwiches, slab cake and lemonade and then races. On other occasions the children piled into a farm wagon swept out and decked with flags and streamers, and were taken to Castle Acre where they ran up and down the ruins, chasing each other in high spirits and carving their names on the stone. The simple food was served from hampers and afterwards they had a group photograph taken. On one occasion, in 1912, Eliza decided to splash out on a snapshot of her three children as well, both of which have survived the years. When it grew dusk, they climbed back on the wagon and the horses drew them slowly and sleepily homeward, their once-clean clothes rumpled and grass-stained.

Lying side by side in bed after they came home, the children would relive every minute, their voices at first a mere whisper, but growing louder and more excited as they recounted the best bits. At last their father would holler up the stairs with his familiar 'Howd yar nize t'gether' and they would fall silent. But they were too exhilarated to sleep and pulled the covers up over their heads to continue talking.

and they were welcome to those during the day. The best ones were for keeping and, besides, eating in bed was not allowed.

They crept across the creaking floor, opened the cupboard and groped about in the dark for an apple each. Thump. Doris dropped hers and they stood stock-still with their hearts in their mouths as it rolled across the floor.

'Wha's agoo'n on up there?' Their father's voice drifted up to them.

They stifled their laughter. 'The bed knob fell off,' Doris called back.

'Do yer want me up there arter yer? Git yarselves back inta bed and don't let me hear no more on yer, dew yer'll be hully sorry.' Doris retrieved the fallen apple and they crept back between the sheets.

'The trouble was,' my mother told me, 'we didn't know what to do with the cores and ended up eating them, but I'm sure the bed was full of pips next morning.'

Whit Sunday was another red-letter day at the Chapel. It was called 'The Anniversary', and on that day, the children were expected to stand up and recite a verse to the whole congregation. If they got through it without making a mistake, they were awarded a book. These books, inscribed with the date and their names, contained stories of a highly moral and very sentimental nature and were treasured by the children, for whom a book was a luxury. When each child married and left home, they took their books with them, but Aunt Norah had never married and her Sunday School books were still at the cottage when I was a child. When the weather was wet and I was at a loose end, I was given some of them to read, but I found the sentiment too cloying.

Gladys, Doris and Alfred, 1912.

'Let's have an apple,' Alfred suggested once.

Their mother used the cupboard at the head of the stairs in their room for storing the pick of the season's fruit. The apples were laid out on the shelves, polished and carefully spaced apart and the children knew they were not supposed to touch them. If they wanted an apple, there were plenty of windfalls in a bucket in the shed

But the big day of the year was Whit Monday. The Whitsuntide revelry at Necton dated back to medieval times when various 'purse clubs' or benefit societies, organised the proceedings and provided prizes for 'gamesters' who were skilful with cudgels and back-swords. The winners were those who could break the most heads in combat. Breaking heads meant shaving off a little skin and drawing blood. Those who suffered this indignity were awarded a consolation prize of a shilling. Each year it became more and more boisterous until Major Mason, an ancestor of the Squire, decided enough was enough and intervened. In 1817, he began providing a more civilised holiday programme. It became the Necton Guild for Rural Sports, held on Whit Monday every year.

The festivities took place in a field opposite Necton Hall grounds. On a mound in the centre of the field a maypole was erected and around it were stalls and booths offering games and refreshments. The biggest booth was decorated in honour of an individual who had been appointed 'Mayor of the Guild' and was reserved for him and his entourage.

Early on Whit Monday afternoon, a procession formed led by the local constable wearing a red scarf, followed by the beadle and the children who were going to dance round the maypole. There was a band (Necton was renowned for its fine musicians), followed by sword bearers and standard bearers and the Mayor of the Guild, mounted on a splendid horse and wearing purple robes and a chain of office. He was followed by the mayor-elect also on horseback, and other dignitaries, and then Morris dancers. When they arrived at the

entrance to the Hall, they were met by the Squire. After the speeches, during which the Mayor relinquished his office and the Mayor Elect took over, the procession returned to the field where the fun began.

There was wrestling, sprinting, sack races, wheelbarrow races and for the less athletic there were side stalls and hoopla, guess the weight of the cake and the number of peas in a jar as well as sticking the tail on the donkey. The men bowled for a pig and, unlike similar competitions nowadays, the pig was alive and squealing. In those hard up times it was a prize worth striving for. In the evening a dance was held in the Mayor's booth. The Necton Guild became famous and people came from far and wide to take part. It was still being held well into this century, though by the time I came on the scene the procession had been discontinued and it became an ordinary village fête.

In May 1910, the country was thrown into mourning when Edward VII died of pneumonia. There was a special memorial service at Necton church on Friday 20 May, attended by almost the whole village. The Necton Lodge of the Oddfellows turned out to a man and marched through the village headed by the village band, which had performed so cheerfully at the Whitsun Fair, now playing mournful music. They were met at the lychgate by the choir, who led them into the packed church for the service. As it ended a peel of muffled bells broke out over the stillness of the countryside, to be echoed in Holme Hale, Bradenham, Pickenham, Dunham, Dereham and Swaffham, and indeed across the whole land.

Walter was working out in the fields when he heard them. He looked up and doffed his

The Mothers' Union.

"What therefore God hath joined together, let not man put asunder."—*St. Mark* x, 9.

MEMBER'S CARD.   (*Revised* 1912.)

Objects.

1.—To uphold the Sanctity of Marriage.
2.—To awaken in Mothers of all Classes a sense of their great responsibility in the training of their boys and girls (the future Fathers and Mothers of the Empire).
3.—To organise in every place a band of Mothers who will unite in prayer and seek by their own example to lead their families in purity and holiness of life.

I DESIRE to acknowledge that by my marriage vow I have pledged myself to love, to help, and to be faithful to my Husband till death us do part.

I DESIRE to remember that my Children have been made Members of our Lord Jesus Christ in Holy Baptism, and dedicated body and soul to His Service, and that it is my duty so to train them that they may continue His faithful Soldiers and Servants unto their lives' end.

I DESIRE BY GOD'S HELP—

1. To guard my Home, to the utmost of my power, from the dangers of Infidelity, Impurity, Intemperance, Betting, and Gambling.
2. To teach my children to pray daily, to read the Bible with them, especially the four Gospels, and to instruct them in our Holy Christian Faith.
3. To lead them to hallow God's Day, and to worship Him regularly in His House of Prayer.
4. To train my children to be obedient, truthful, pure, self-controlled and industrious, and to set them a good example in word and deed.
5. To guard them from bad and doubtful companions, influences, and amusements, and to discourage slander and gossip in my Home.
6. To be very careful as to the books, periodicals, and papers which they read, and which are seen in my Home.
7. To encourage a spirit of reverence by precept and example.

GOD grant that I may so use the means of Grace, that united to our Lord Jesus Christ, and abiding in Him I may be enabled to fulfil my duty as a faithful Wife and a wise and loving Mother.

Special Prayer for Communicant Members.

GOD grant that I may so use the means of Grace, that united to God through our Lord Jesus Christ, and being continually strengthened and refreshed with the spiritual Food of His most Blessed Body and Blood, I may fulfil my duty as a faithful Wife and a wise and loving Mother in the power of the Holy Spirit. Amen.

The Mothers' Union Prayer to be said daily.

O LORD, fill us with Thy Holy Spirit, that we may firmly believe in JESUS CHRIST, and love Him with all our hearts. Wash our souls in His Precious Blood. Make us to hate sin, and to be holy in thought, word and deed. Help us to be faithful wives and loving mothers. Bless us and all who belong to the Mothers' Union, unite us together in love and prayer, and teach us to train our children for Heaven. Pour out Thy Holy Spirit on our husbands and child. Make our Homes Homes of peace and love, and may we so live on earth that may live with Thee for ever in Heaven; for JESUS CHRIST'S sake. Amen.

"As for me and my house, we will serve the Lord. *Joshua* x   5

"I am the Vine, ye are the Branches : He that abideth in Me, and I in him, the same bringeth forth much fruit : for without Me ye can do nothing."—St. John xv, 5.

"Blessed are the pure in heart, for they shall see God." St. Matthew v, 8.

Eliza's Mothers' Union card.

hat in respect, then continued plodding between the rows of emerging crops with his long-handled weed hook, chopping at the thistles, the poppies and the dock with a strong rhythmic movement designed to keep him going for hours on end.

Eliza was a stalwart member of the Mother's Union, and was always ready to help with whatever project they had going. She would meet Maud Powley and Vi Fickling at the top of the Drift and together they would walk to the meetings, held in a room at the Good Woman before the village hall was built. One year they entertained the inhabitants with singing and sketches. There was also a Friendship Club, started by Miss Hilda Mason, the Squire's daughter. Hilda said it was not fair that the men should get together at the pub and have their drink and smokes and put the world to rights while the women were left at home and so she formed the club for the women. They would take their knitting or sewing and enjoy a good gossip over a cup of tea and sometimes they had outings to places of interest.

I think Miss Mason might have had some sympathy for the suffragettes, who were making a name for themselves about this time by organising rallies and demonstrations in Hyde Park, chaining themselves to railings and being force fed in prison. When, in 1911, posters went up in Swaffham advertising a visit by the suffragette van from which a leading exponent of women's suffrage was billed to speak, my grandmother and her friends could not resist going to hear what she had to say. To the huge amusement of the men and the chagrin of the women, the van did not turn up and the whole meeting ended in anticli-

max. As far as Walter was concerned, it served the women right. He believed they should keep their proper place and that was at home under the dominance of their menfolk. He insisted Grandma agreed with him and, smiling, she always said she did, but only in his hearing, of course.

In February 1912, the temperature dropped as low as -35°F and many died from the cold, which was made worse by a strike by the mineworkers. The strike only ended after the Government had agreed to the principle of a minimum wage, but shortly afterwards the country was in the grip of dock and transport strikes. Nothing could be done on the land and life was looking very bleak indeed.

It was about this time that Eliza heard from her sister, Alice, that Frank Ringwood, the man she had hoped to marry, had decided to emigrate to Canada. Many people were emigrating at that time, hoping for better opportunities abroad, but she had not thought he really meant it. Now he had gone and Alice was feeling very low and thinking of following him. Eliza wrote her a comforting letter, but she could not bring herself to encourage her sister to go. It was such a long way and if things did not work out, she would be thousands of miles from home and family. Eliza herself would miss her, even though they rarely had the opportunity to meet. But Alice could not envisage life without the man she loved and in spite of Eliza's misgivings, made up her mind to go. She wrote to tell Eliza she had used all her savings to book a berth on the *Titanic*.

There was a lot of publicity about this liner, which was getting ready for its maiden voyage in April. Although it was a glittering example of luxury travel with staterooms, cocktail bars, a glittering ballroom and grand staircase, it was also an immigrant ship and berths in the third class steerage could be had for £9. With sixteen watertight compartments it was said to be unsinkable and this gave Eliza some comfort. She was hoping to see Alice one last time before she went, but as she was once again pregnant and very big, even at five months, she decided not to travel.

A family death caused Alice to postpone her departure, which Eliza said was the hand of providence when the unthinkable happened and the *Titanic* went down on 15 April. More than a thousand passengers and crew perished. Although she was heartily thankful for her lucky escape, Alice was still determined to go and began making new plans.

But at least she was still in England when, on the 9 June Eliza gave birth to twins, Emma Lyle and Norah Ellen, and she was able to visit and offer her congratulations. Almost sensing that they were about to part forever, the two women hugged and kissed and promised to write. Eliza and Alice were alike in many ways; they were both intelligent and practical and accepted stoically whatever fate doled out to them, the good and the bad. Both were loyal and loving, and they had a terrific sense of humour that stood them in good stead when life became difficult.

And for Eliza, it was difficult. There were now six children and hardly more money to feed them than when Walter and Eliza were first married. The Ong farm was just holding its own, but David was 72 and though he was entitled to draw his old age pension of 5 shillings a week, it was hardly enough to allow him to give up work. He still needed the income from the smallholding and Walter found himself taking more and more of the work on his own shoulders, though he was still working for Mr Adcock at Chapel Farm.

They paid their bills and held their heads up in the community, but there were days when Eliza wondered where the next meal was coming from. Nothing was ever wasted. They grew what food they could and made good use of the bounty of the fields and hedgerows: blackberries, elderberries, mushrooms. Rabbits, moorhens and pigeons, all went into the pot. It was better than asking for charitable relief.

Charity meant a visit from the Relieving Officer and proclaimed to everyone that Walter was not man enough to help himself and his family. 'We pay our way and allus hev done,' he would say. 'So long as we've got a bit o' bread and cheese and a roof over our heads, we'll manage.' Bread and cheese and water were all that was needed to sustain life, he maintained, and who was to say he was not right?

Then, on 4 August 1914, the conflict began that was to become known as the 'war to end all wars' and life changed for everyone.

The Countryside at War

THERE HAD been rumblings of trouble for some time, but it all seemed far away and not particularly relevant to the ordinary people in Britain, certainly not to Walter and Eliza, who were busy bringing up their children. They knew the country had begun quietly calling up reserves – territorials who had joined simply to earn a few extra shillings and take a fortnight's holiday at the taxpayers' expense. The possibility that they might have to fight had not come into it, but when things came to a head with the assassination of Archduke Franz Ferdinand in Sarajevo in 1914 everyone, including the people of Necton, was forced to face reality.

In a patriotic fervour, thousands of young men went cheerfully off to fight with bands playing and flags flying, and Norfolk men were no exception. Dozens of families gathered in the railway yard in Swaffham to wave their menfolk off. Walter, at 42, was too old to go to war and his children too young, so no one in the immediate family joined up, although Aunt Sarah Crockley's eldest son, William, went and so did John Stibbon who had married Walter's sister, Florence. Maybe he thought, as many others did, that it would mean a regular wage and allowances and

perhaps the pundits would be right and it would not last beyond Christmas.

Just before Christmas, with no end to the war in sight, Eliza learned that Alice's wedding had taken place. The following year their beloved Grandmother Brown died in Swaffham at the age of 84. She had had 'a good innings', as my grandmother put it, but it was still a sad blow. She had been a second mother to Eliza and Alice, giving them the love and affection that had been so necessary to two grieving little girls. Apart from Benjamin, the old lady had been Eliza's last link with the Brown family and after her death she rarely spoke of them. But life, and the war, had to go on and by then Eliza herself was pregnant again.

It was the Zeppelins that worried them most. They were like great silver cigars, over 400ft long, with two cars suspended beneath them. The early ones did not have the range to reach London, their eventual target, but odd ones were seen off the east coast at the beginning of the war. These sightings were reported in all the newspapers and were added to and embroidered on by the population, whose fears were very real indeed.

'We hear a noise in the distance and see shapes in the sky and we look at each other and say, "Them Zepps are coming."' Grandma told me, as we washed up after our midday meal in the summer of 1939. The other children had disappeared as soon as they were allowed to leave the table, Aunt Norah had gone on the bus to do some shopping in Swaffham and Grandad had returned to whatever he was busy with outside, so I could quiz my grandmother without anyone interrupting. 'But they didn't come, not at first, and we begin to think it was all a fairy tale and they couldn't get here. We soon learn different.'

It was East Anglia, and Norfolk in particular, that bore the brunt of the early attacks. On Christmas morning 1914, a solitary machine dropped two bombs and quickly left. Three weeks later, two more crossed the Norfolk coast and dropped their bombs anywhere they saw a concentration of lights. London had a half-hearted blackout, but there was little restriction in the country. Places like King's Lynn, Norwich and Great Yarmouth were still well-lit and damage and casualties were reported in all these places.

It was the first time civilians had been attacked in war and the raids had a demoralising effect, especially as the small biplanes, sent up to do battle with them, were not having much success. Civilians on the ground could not know the difficulties of being forewarned soon enough to get the planes airborne from their tarpaulin hangars in the stubble fields and at a sufficient altitude to intercept the enemy airships before they reached their target; they only knew that the Zeppelins appeared to fly over unmolested.

The route of one of the monsters was traced from Bacton, where it crossed the coast, to Cromer, Sheringham, Beeston, Brancaster, Hunstanton, Snettisham and King's Lynn, bombing as it went. There was damage to buildings and several casualties. News soon reached Necton, which is only 20 or so miles from King's Lynn, and the following morning groups of excited people stood about discussing the raid and wondering aloud who would be next.

'There was an unexploded bomb in a hedge at Pickenham,' Grandma told me. 'We walked over to look at the hole it made.'

She paused to take the bowl of washing up water out of the door and throw it in a wide arc over the garden before wiping the inside of the bowl, upending it on the table in the back place and coming back indoors. 'Everyone was talking about the raids,' she went on as she dried the tray we had been using as a draining board and gave it to me to put in the cupboard, before wiping down the oil cloth on the table and settling down to some mending while I listened enthralled. 'Some say they see the Zepps, others say they only hear 'em, and there were all sorts of squit about them landing and leaving spies behind.'

At the beginning of World War I, Norfolk had been obsessed with spy mania. One story went the rounds that car lights were being used to signal to the enemy. If that was the case, they were surprisingly unsuccessful in pinpointing strategic targets; it was generally ordinary town buildings and civilians that were hit.

'They were so big and they flew over so low,' my mother told me later. 'I was only 10 at the time and terrified out of my life. We could hear their engines a long way off and we'd lay in bed and hold our breath as they came nearer and nearer. The cats used to run and hide and the dogs set up a howl. Sometimes the noise faded and you knew they'd turned away, but sometimes they came right overhead. We expected them to drop their bombs right on top of us and then we tumbled out of bed and scrambled underneath. When they'd gone over, we giggled with relief and ran to the window to see if we could see them going.'

During these times, the intrepid Walter, carrying a shielded storm lantern, made his way round the outbuildings, pigsties, stables and cowsheds, to see that the farm animals were all right. Grandma was left in the house, doing her knitting, waiting for the birth of her next child. Audrey Joan was born on the 18 August 1915, completing their family of five girls and two boys.

There were more raids in the following month. On the 15 September one machine had engine trouble and wallowed over Norfolk most of the night trying to correct it, before abandoning its main target and jettisoning its bombs over East Dereham, less than eight miles from Necton. 'That was the biggest fright we had,' my mother said. 'It was far too close for comfort.'

The bombs damaged two or three houses and killed four men. There were seven or eight injured too, including some women. Next morning a bundle of German newspapers, part of a German officer's uniform and a leave pass were found in a meadow at Scarning, a village on the Necton side of East Dereham, giving rise to more spy stories. My mother-in-law, who lived in Scarning and was 13 at the time, told me it was possible to make out the faces of the German crew as it flew low over the rooftops.

While Zeppelin raids were large in the minds of the people and could be seen and heard, there were other theatres of war that took their toll of agricultural communities like Necton.

In the Eastern Counties, if not in other places, cattle had always been the most important animals on the farm. They provided milk and meat, as well as manure, so it is hardly surprising that the main crop was grass, either temporary or permanent pasture, and much of the acreage under the plough at the beginning of the war was used to grow food for animals. Grain for the country's bread came from the great prairies of America. But in 1915 changes were taking place in farming that would never be reversed; the farmers were being exhorted to plough up their pasture and sow wheat.

Older farmers remembered the long years of depression when the price of grain had fallen through the floor and they did not want to see it happen again. They were reluctant to obey the directives without some guarantees. Knowing they could not feed the country without the co-operation of the farmers, the government guaranteed the price, which would vary from year to year according to yields. This may have encouraged farmers to plough up uncultivated land, but it was not easy without labour, horses, machinery and fertiliser, all of which were soon hard to come by as ships were sunk by enemy action and more and more were taken over for transporting troops, ammunition, horses and fodder to France.

It was not only the 'plough up' campaign that caused resentment. Advice and instruction arrived by post on every aspect of the farm: drainage, pest control, the growing of all sorts of foodstuffs besides cereals, the distribution of feed and supplies, and the sale of farm horses, which was strictly controlled. Financial help was also arranged when farmers needed credit to buy seed and supplies against future yields.

'The farmers hatta fill in forms and some on 'em spent hours trying to make sense on 'em.' my grandmother told me, pushing a wooden mushroom into one of John's socks to reveal an enormous hole. Nowadays we would throw the sock away, but she would not have dreamed of doing so while it could be mended. She set to work, darning in and out, talking as she did so. 'Some just tuck them behind the clock on the mantel and forget all about them but they hatta do them in the end.'

There was a committee or board for almost every commodity and clubs set up for rearing pigs and keeping poultry. With these came the attendant regulations and showers of leaflets.

'Nigh on everyone kept a pig,' my grandmother said. 'A pig kin live off scraps and ha' two litters a year and after you butcher it, you kin use it all from the head to the trotters, there's no waste. When you killed a pig, you were let keep half of it, the rest had to go to the butcher, though they do say that you shouldn't slaughter a pig when the moon is waxing, dew the bacon will run to fat in the pan.'

I had seen her boiling up half a head and a couple of trotters in a huge pan with herbs and seasoning and then straining the resultant glutinous mess and carefully picking out the little pieces of meat, which she put in the strained liquid before pour-

ing it into basins to set. The resulting brawn was delicious eaten cold with salad.

Orders were issued for the control of rabbits, rooks and rats, and farmers were also asked to organise pigeon shoots and take action against sparrows. 'I recollect there was a bounty of a shilling a dozen for rats' tails,' Grandma went on, 'three pence a dozen for the heads of fully-fledged sparrows and a penny a dozen for sparrow eggs.'

'But I thought you weren't supposed to raid birds' nests?' I said, remembering the statue of the one-armed boy and my grandmother's frequent instructions to my brother never to take more than one egg from a nest and always to make sure there were others left. 'Birds can't count,' she would tell him, 'but if you leave the nest empty, then they'll know.'

Now she said, 'This was wartime. Seems the government can do what it likes in wartime.'

Most farmers complied with the directives, in spite of their misgivings, and the acreage of wheat went up by 20 per cent in the first year of the war, the highest it had been since 1891, the year my grandmother had arrived in Necton.

It was a good harvest that year in spite of a very wet season, which had delayed the ploughing and drilling. The price of corn exceeded the guaranteed price set by the government, but this was more than offset by the increase in income tax from 1s 8d in the pound to 3 shillings. Small farmers rarely kept detailed accounts, often doing no more than totting up income and expenditure, mostly to see if they could afford to buy the children new shoes, some new piece of equipment or increase their flock or herd. Because this was well-known and nothing would make the died-in-the-wool farmer change his habits to please the bureaucrats, a tenant farmer's income had been assessed by the Inland Revenue as one third of his rent, but now it was deemed to be the equivalent of his full annual rent.

People like David Ong, who was long past retirement age but still working, were assessed on the rent their property might be assumed to fetch and he did not see how he was going to find the extra money to pay the tax man. It should not have affected Walter, who was still employed as a labourer on Chapel Farm, but as he was doing a large share of the work on the smallholding too (his younger brother had been lured to London by the prospect of better wages and had become a tram driver), he was at the sharp end of his parents' grumbling, especially that of his mother, who seemed to think he had several pairs of hands.

The farmers' problems were made all the more difficult because in Norfolk over a third of the male population between the ages of 18 and 40 had left for military service or had gone to build airfields, which were proliferating all over East Anglia. 'The wages for that were higher than any they could get working on the land,' my grandmother said.

For those who stayed behind, there was more than enough work and a labourer's wages rose to 18 shillings a week and then 25 shillings. This was more than they had ever earned before, but prices rose even more steeply. The price of a loaf of bread went up in the first year of the war from 4½d to 7d and in the second year to 8¼d and later to 9d. People were exhorted not to waste bread. 'As if we would,' Grandma said. 'Not with bread at that price.'

Leaflets were issued like confetti, telling housewives what to cook and how to cook it. I sensed that she had been almost as incensed over that as Grandad had been over the Agricultural directives. So much of their early lives had revolved around finding enough to eat that economising was second nature to her. 'Waste not, want not,' she would say when I turned my nose up at something on my plate.

She put down her mending and went into the other room to root about in the cupboard next to the hearth where she kept all her treasures. She came back with a couple of pieces of yellowing paper, which she handed to me to read. One was a copy of a leaflet issued by the Ministry of Food and was called Mr Slice o' Bread:

I am a slice of bread. I measure three inches by two and a half and my thickness is half an inch. My weight is exactly one ounce. I am wasted once a day by 48,000,000 people of Britain. I am the 'bit left over', the slice eaten absent-mindedly when really I wasn't needed: I am the waste crust.

If you collected me and my companions for a whole week, you would find that we amounted to 9,380 tons of good bread – WASTED! Nine shiploads of good bread! Almost as much as twenty German submarines could sink – even if they had good luck. When you throw me away or waste me, you are adding twenty submarines to the German navy. Save me and I will save you!

'I did hear of a man being fined £5 for feeding bread crumbs to the ducks,' Grandma told me, gazing out of the open back door towards the orchard. Half a dozen plump ducks waddled towards the gate to the garden. I guessed Grandad was somewhere about with a feed pail.

The other piece of paper had been cut from a woman's magazine and was a recipe for wartime soup, which no one today, nor even in 1939 when I was talking to her of it, would contemplate eating. It consisted of saving all the outer leaves of cabbage, cauliflower, broccoli, lettuce, leeks and onions and the tops and tails of turnips, carrots, parsnips and swedes, together with the leftovers in saucepans and dishes, bread crusts, the remains of suet puddings, savoury sauces, cheese and bacon rinds, gravy and vegetable water, all of which were boiled up together, and seasoned, before putting in a haybox for two or three hours and then put through a sieve before serving. 'Grandad's pigs had better fare,' she said.

'What's a haybox?' I asked.

'It's a wooden box packed with hay. It makes its own heat and you can put a saucepan or a dish in it to cook things like stews that need long, slow cooking. It saves fuel. That was another thing we were short of. We made briquettes with coal dust, clay and sawdust,' She laughed suddenly. 'I never thought learning to make bricks would come in useful again.'

'There used to be meetings up at the village hall and people would come and tell us how to economise on food,' she went on. 'They shew us how to make rissoles out of scraps of bacon, cold meat, left over vegetables and stale bread minced up together and mixed with oatmeal and vegetable stock. One time we were told to eat more potatoes because there was a glut and the very next year the crop failed and we were told to eat

ground maize or flaked rice instead, neither of which we grow ourselves.'

She was a very good cook, nothing fancy of course, but plain wholesome food made as tasty as it was possible to make it. I never saw her use a recipe book and there was not a pair of scales in sight. She knew by looking at a pat of butter, a cup of flour or sugar, just how much it weighed. 'I've done it so often, I don't need to weigh it,' she told me when I questioned her about it. But she did let me into a secret, ½lb of margarine is easily divided in two or four to make 4 or 2oz, a tablespoon of flour is 1oz, while 1oz of sugar is a rounded dessert spoonful and a teacup of milk is 1⅓pt. 'So, if the recipe says ½lb of flour, how many tablespoons, do you need?' she would ask, and in this way I had a simple arithmetic lesson.

She was adept at making a little go a long way and she could produce such mouth-watering gravy that I would have been content with that and a piece of bread to soak in it, not realising that on many occasions, my mother and her siblings had to make do with just that when they were children. 'If we had a little bit of meat, Father always had it because he was the breadwinner and he needed the nourishment,' my mother once told me.

There was a little snow in November, followed by dull skies with rain and hail and the rest of the winter was mild but very wet, so that when spring came, the fields were sodden and it was almost impossible to get on to the land. Out in France, the troops were floundering in a sea of mud and dying by the thousand. The lists of those killed in action published in the newspapers was growing longer and longer. The women left at home pored over the names, praying that their loved ones would not be among them.

The summer and autumn continued wet and the 1916 harvest was poor. The expected increase in home food production did not materialise, while the shortage of labour to work the land was even more acute. The farmers wanted boys who were nearly old enough to leave school to be allowed to go early and many of them did. Even the younger ones were often kept at home to lend a hand. Truancy became almost as big a problem as it had been when Grandad was a boy.

The government recognised the difficulty by instructing recruiting parties not to take skilled men from the farms, but that policy went by the board when conscription was introduced. At first recruits had to be 5ft 8ins tall, but this was soon reduced to 5ft 5ins and then 5ft 3ins as men were lost and more were needed. A compromise was reached and Agricultural Companies were formed composed of men of medical category C3, 'unfit for service in the army' who were made available for work on the land for the duration of the war.

'The men still working on the farms were none too happy when the soldiers come,' Grandma told me. 'They hatta be paid six shillings a day if they found their own board and lodging and four and sixpence if they live in, and they got sixpence an hour overtime. They did not hev to find their own clothes and their wives got a separation allowance. For doing the work of a labourer, they get as much as a shepherd or a horseman, is it any wonder the men were aggrieved?'

'Useless most on 'em,' said my grandfather, who had just come in from outside.

'They tek our good men and our hosses and then send us others who're about as much use as that there cat.' The cat was fast asleep on the cushion in his chair. He bent down and gave its rump a sharp nudge, making it topple off the chair and tear out of the door. 'Arse about face,' he went on, sitting down in the chair and removing his boots. 'They shoulda let our men alone.' He was not referring to the smallholding in Black Drift because David did not hire labourers, but Chapel Farm where he was employed at the time.

They could try and employ women, but the women, enjoying more freedom and independence than they had ever had before, preferred more lucrative forms of employment. In towns they were working as shop assistants, waitresses and clerks; they drove delivery carts and worked on the railways, jobs that had previously been done by men. And if they wanted to be more directly involved with the war effort, they could become nurses or drive ambulances or work in munitions factories. Even those who stayed at home found ways to earn more money than they would on the land. 'Some on 'em took in the soldiers who were working on the farms,' my grandmother said. 'Their men were in the army and they had their separation allowance and children's allowance, and if they sleep in the room with their children, they had room for a lodger.' She smiled suddenly. 'That's what they said they did, and mayhap they did, but it was funny how many found themselves in the family way when their men hadn't been on leave in months.' This was a rare indiscretion on my grandmother's part; she seemed to have forgotten I was only a child.

'Any old how, the farmers say they'd rather have one man than six women. They say the women weren't strong enough and their skirts get in the way and they were afraid the men would forget theirselves and use bad language in front on 'em.'

In spite of that, 45,000 women from all walks of life rushed to offer their services when the Women's Land Army was formed. The selection committees favoured the more educated among them and paid more attention to character and high moral standards, than suitability and physical fitness, and only 5,000 were accepted. One wonders what their criteria could possibly have been when 40,000 were considered unsuitable.

Those that were enlisted had to overcome the anti-female prejudice which my grandmother had spoken of and a fear on the part of the farmers that if they accepted the women's labour, then they would lose even more men to the armed forces. But as she said, 'Needs must when the devil drives' and before long the women of the WLA were hard at work. Sometimes they lived in barracks and were taken to the farms each day under supervision, but in isolated places, they were billeted on the farms where they worked. They wore a military style uniform and were paid 8 shillings a week, as much as a skilled labourer had been paid at the beginning of the war.

'They did hoeing and weeding, milking, fruit picking, cutting cabbages, picking potatoes,' she said. 'They could drive tractors and shock sheaves as fast as the men.'

The New Year of 1917, the third year of the war, began with severe frost and snow. It was March before the farmers could even begin to think of ploughing, a job that

women did not traditionally do, and when, at last, they were able to make a start, they needed more men and needed them urgently. A contest developed between the Board of Agriculture and the War Office; one wanted the men released to work on the land and the other said the men were needed at the front. It was a battle the Board of Agriculture partially won. Furloughs were given to a number of soldiers recruited from rural districts to go home to help with the ploughing and they obeyed with alacrity.

The trouble was that not many of them had any experience of ploughing, which was a skilled job according to my grandfather. Some statistics I discovered recently pointed out that of 40 men sent home, two had a little experience, four were general farm workers and the rest, including a dustman, merely had experience with horses. 'You couldn't knock narthin' into 'em,' was one comment.

Owing to bad weather the season was late starting and the few tractors that were available were too heavy for the land and in any case kept breaking down. The work was not finished by the end of April when the men were due to go back. Their leave was extended until the middle of May. By this time haymaking was not far off and more men came back in June to cut the hay and later to bring in the harvest, but there were not enough of them.

There was talk of using prisoners of war, but many country people, conditioned by propaganda and tales of atrocities in Europe, believed the Hun was a monster and were terrified of the idea. Highly embroidered tales of escaped prisoners of war were often passed from man to man in pubs, shops and smithies, which was where Walter was when he heard about the two who were on the run from Redington in Suffolk. 'They're heading this way,' he was told. 'Better warn yar folks.' News of the escape sent women and children hurrying to bolt themselves indoors and the men to go warily about their business with half their attention on nearby woods and railway lines. They were thankful when they heard the two had been recaptured at Swaffham and allowed themselves to be taken without a fight.

However, POWs were eventually employed on the land and many of them proved to be good workers and very human after all. To begin with they were kept in camps and sent out in gangs each day under armed guard, but later, when a farmer only wanted the services of one or two to replace men who had enlisted, they were billeted on the farms with the farmer himself responsible for security. They became a common sight around Necton along with the land girls and the soldiers.

Peace at Last

WHILE THE WAR dragged on and the losses mounted, Eliza, with Audrey a baby, was kept busy looking after her family. There was little time or inclination for amusement, although the children still played their traditional games, unconcerned by what was happening in faraway France.

'What did the children do in the war?' I asked my grandmother as more and more talk of a new war impinged on our summer holiday.

'Same as they do now,' she said with a smile. 'Get into mischief, just as you do.'

'But they still went to school?'

'Course they did, those that were old enough, but they hatta do their bit for the war effort. They were paid thruppence a pound for picking rose hips and blackberries. The rose hips were made into syrup and the blackberries into jam and jelly and sent out to the soldiers. They collected acorns and beech nuts for pig feed, and horse chestnuts, which were wanted in the munitions factories but I don't know what for.'

Queues for food stretched endlessly. Imports of sugar were strictly limited and the country had to rely on home-grown sugar beet, which had to compete with the general need for wheat. Consequently sugar disappeared off the grocers' shelves. 'Would you believe there were some people who thought you'd die if you didn't have at least a pound of sugar a week?' my grandmother told me. 'Why, if that were true, we'd all hev bin in our graves years afore. We couldn't afford to buy it when we were young.'

'How did you sweeten things then?'

'We didn't have a lot of sweet stuff and there was honey, much better for you, and treacle until everyone got wise to that and it got as scarce as sugar. They didn't have rationing until nearly the end of the war, and then sugar was one o' the first things to be rationed.'

'What's rationing mean?' I asked, not realising that before very long I would be experiencing it myself.

'It's a way of making sure that everybody have a fair share of what's going when everything's hard to come by. The sugar ration was 8oz a week and you hatta be registered with a grocer for it and when things got short he wouldn't sell you anything unless you were registered with him for sugar and then you couldn't just have sugar, you had to buy something else as well. And when the price of evrathing go up, there was price control. I recall 1lb of butter were one and sixpence, margarine eightpence. It was ninepence for cheese, one and sixpence for bacon. Sugar was fourpence ha'penny. A chicken cost half a crown.'

'That's not very much,' I said.

'It was a lot that time o' day. It wasn't only food shortages, fuel, paper, leather and even wool for our knitting was hard to come by,' She chuckled suddenly. 'Do you know it were illegal to throw rice at a wedding and you couldn't put starch in your laundry? And if you go into Swaffham on market day and go in a tea-shop for a cuppa and a bite, you'd only be let have a titty[18] bit of cake, no bigger'n a matchbox. Proper rationing didn't come in until nearly the end of the war. Then the grown ups were allowed 1½lb of meat a week and the children 10oz. Butter and marg was 4oz a week.'

I was sitting beside her while she knitted a sock by the light of an oil lamp. Earlier she had taught me how to do garter stitch and a kind of double loop stitch and I had two stumpy wooden needles and a ball of fine string with which I optimistically hoped to knit a dishcloth as a Christmas present for my mother. John had already gone to bed and it would be my turn in half an hour, but until then, I made the most of my private time with my grandmother.

'Everyone knitted in those days,' she told me. 'Not only women, but men and children too, until we couldn't get wool any more. We used to collect the fleece snagged on the hedges and barbed wire. If you got enough, you could spin it and dye it, but it take a lot and the farmers weren't keepin' so many sheep cos the land was most all ploughed up.'

But the 'plough up' campaign had not been as successful as the government had hoped and additional incentives were needed. County War Agricultural Committees were formed under the auspices of the Food Production Department who appointed local Executive Committees consisting of farmers, landowners and land agents, plus a member of the Board of Agriculture and,

in Norfolk, a trade union leader. Officers from these bodies were sent out to survey the farms.

'They class the farms into three kinds,' she went on. 'Those that were well-farmed, those that could be improved, and some they call derelict, which were a bit hard on the farmers. If the farmer was a tenant, and he didn't pull his socks up, they got the landowner to end the tenancy. The land was took over by the Committee and they put a farm manager in.'

'I shouldn't think the farmers thought much of that,' I said.

'No, some on 'em were fare savage. They didn't like people poking their noses in their business, but they got their own back and hev a good laugh when they see the new managers struggle to make a go of a farm that weren't ever going to come to ennathing.'

'What about the good farmers?'

'Oh, they were give advice on how to improve and told which meadows to plough up and sow with crops. They told Grandad's Pa to plough up the calf medder and that weren't above a couple of acres.'

'It were grass ever since anyone kin remember,' he grumbled. 'They didn't tek into account that medders are medders and it tek more than a year to put new ploughed land into good heart. It oon't grow good crops the first year, nor yet the second. And ev'raone say the war'd be over afore it do a bit o' good. And what did they think the calves were going to live on? Feed were hard enough to come by without that.'

Apart from the appalling loss of men, it was the plight of the horses that worried Walter most about the war, not only

[18]tiny

because he was being deprived of their use, but because he hated the thought of them being shot to pieces on the battlefield. 'You should see them they send back, good for narthin' but the knacker's yard,' he said. 'They kin't bear to hear yer holler and if yer was to crack a gun nigh on 'em, they'd be off into the next shere, and no stoppin' 'em. What good's a hoss like that?'

The Director of Remounts was buying 3,000 horses a day: hunters for riding and draught horses to pull carts and guns. They were supposed to come from urban and industrial sources, but there were never enough and the farms lost a large proportion of their animals too. Breeding was intensified as farmers tried to satisfy the needs of the army and replenish their own stocks, and mares were often covered again only nine or ten days after giving birth. Mares treated in this way did not last long and they could not be put to work. 'Poor beasts,' Walter said. 'That's no way to treat a good hoss.'

The horses left behind had to work harder and with good fodder at a premium that was difficult. 'A team of two hosses kin work nigh on 50 acres,' Grandad explained. 'But you can't cut a hoss in two and you hev to hev one even if you've only got five acres. And it hatta be fed.'

At the height of the war, fodder was being shipped to France at the rate of 70,000 tons a month and it was the task of the Forage Corps to obtain it. There would be quite a cavalcade as these men travelled from farm to farm: a horse and wagon with a driver and two others, then a traction engine, a hay baler, a couple of transport wagons, a living van and water cart carrying the water to cool the engine. When

they reached the farm, they set up the machinery in the rickyard and set to work. The hay was compacted into bales of 200lb each and fastened with wire before being loaded on to carts and delivered to the nearest railway station for shipment. No doubt the farmers got a good price for it, but it left them scratching their heads about how to feed their own animals.

Alfred took his leave of the fearsome Mr Stead and left school for the last time in the summer of 1917. It was a time when labour was desperately short and wages were high, as much as 25 shillings a week for a full-grown man. But he was not full-grown, however much he liked to think he was, and Walter looked on him in much the same way as his father had done a generation before, not quite believing that the helpless child he had reared was 13 years old and capable of working on his own, nor that he was able to think for himself.

Alfred, by all accounts was a normal mischievous boy, into everything. He loved being out and about and was full of nervous energy. He liked the farm machinery more than the animals and in his school holidays would follow the steam engine and the binder and reaper as it made its way from farm to farm. He could not wait to get his hands on a tractor. But there were only 66 tractors in the whole of Norfolk at that time and this was a pipe dream. He was put to work on a local farm, learning, just as Walter had done, by watching his elders and betters and doing as he was told.

The usual crop of jokes was played on him by the other men, such as telling him to fetch a rubber mallet or a peck of hurdle seeds. He was a country boy and wise to those but, war or no war, the older men were not going to let him escape the ritual of being turned upside down and held by his ankles by two of them while a third drove a nail into the heel of his boot. He squealed and wriggled about, but he was being held high enough for his hands to be clear of the ground and was virtually helpless.

'Yew gooin' to treat us?' the men laughed. 'A pint of good ale for one and all.'

'No!' shouted Alfred, his face turning red with the flow of blood to his head.

The hammering continued. Alfred's boots were good ones, the soles as thick as Walter and Eliza could afford. His head was buzzing long before he felt the nail in his heel.

'Why, the stubborn fule be a-gooun' to let us do it,' one of his tormentors said. 'Best let him be.'

'That I woon't,' said the man with the hammer. 'He hatta larn and larn him I mean to. I hatta buy my way on to the harvest field when I were a younker and you did an' all, he's no different.'

While they argued, Alfred dangled helplessly, if vociferously. He knew the time-honoured custom and he also knew that if he gave in too easily, he'd never hear the end of it; he had to prove how much of a man he was. He was strong and healthy and had inherited his father's indomitable courage and his mother's obstinacy. The tip of the nail was on his heel before he shouted, 'Beer!', the signal for the men to lower him to the ground and pull out the nail.

'He's a plucky one,' they said, as they pulled off his boot and sock to inspect the damage. 'Come you on, bor, rub a bit o' salt in it and let's get to work.'

And that's how Alfred proved himself a man. When the harvest was finished, he helped with the threshing, done then, as I had seen it done, with a petrol engine out in the open where they were building the new straw stack. When the fields had been ploughed there was seed to be set, not as Walter had done it as a young man, but by machinery, primitive by today's standards perhaps, but effective. He did not follow the plough, the men who did were too proud of their straight furrows to allow a mere stripling to have a hand in that. But there was weeding and hoeing to be done, animals to feed and clean out, and any number of other jobs. In fact, he carried on the family tradition of farming, because, as far as he could see there was no help for it.

The arrival of the Americans at the Western front in the autumn of 1917 was greeted with enthusiasm and hope that at last the fortunes of war would make a turn for the better. At first nothing seemed to change and the loss of life continued; place names few had even heard of before the war, like Mons, Ypres, Passchendale, Verdun, the Marne and the Somme were etched on people's minds. Many men were coming back from the war scarred in mind and body and unable to talk about their experiences. Many a wife, mother or sweetheart wondered what horrors their men had endured to bring on such brooding silences and, at the other end of the scale, unnatural jollity and a tendency to drink too much at a time when a bottle of whisky, which before the war had cost 3s 6d, now cost a staggering 12s 6d.

Eliza was always one to take note of weather conditions; her surviving diary mentions it almost every day and she remembered the new year of 1918 as a time of very severe weather. 'There were eight foot drifts,' she told me, as we sat knitting in the warmth of the kitchen. 'The ice on the pit was six inches thick and the children went on to it with old fen skates fastened to their boots. Grandad hatta keep watch that no one went through.'

Spring arrived at last and once it 'forgive', the weather remained good. But it had its repercussions on the front line when the Germans launched a spring offensive and broke through the allied lines, causing enormous casualties. Everyone was feeling very low and wondering when it would all end.

One day Eliza was summoned by a neighbour rushing down the Drift and shouting, 'Mrs Ong, come quick! Come quick! Leslie Tubby's been and shot his father.'

Mr Tubby, a farmer, lived in a white house opposite the top end of the drift. Eliza, not even questioning why she should be called to the scene, hurried to see what she could do, fearing the worst. He was an intractable and unsociable man and worked his 16-year-old son very hard, allowing him no freedom and she supposed Leslie had simply been goaded beyond endurance. 'Poor Leslie Tubby was a ha'penny short of a shilling,' my grandmother explained. 'He was convinced everyone's hand was ag'in him. He was always frettin' and shoutin' over something and driv the rest of his family near as demented as himself, but we all thought he was harmless.'

How he got hold of his father's gun, no one knows, though I do not suppose it was difficult; shotguns were quite ordinary things for farmers to have about the place for shooting pigeons and rabbits and pheasant too, if you were lucky to be invited on to the Squire's land for a day's sport. They should not have been left about loaded, of course, but the cartridges would not have been kept far away, and Leslie, even in his confused state of mind, was cunning, 'a bit old' was my grandmother's description. Whatever was wrong, Leslie was not articulate enough to tell them. My mother said he thought the Germans were coming and was in a 'right old state', though that does not explain why he should take it into his head to take a pot shot at his father.

The news that Leslie Tubby had run amok and was killing everyone he met spread through the village like wildfire and mothers collected up their children and hurried indoors. Who restrained the young lad, I do not know; he was probably frightened by all the fuss. Fortunately the wound, though severe, was not fatal and Mr Tubby lived to tell the tale and Leslie was put into a mental home.

About this time old Mrs Yaxley, mother of my grandfather's great friend, Bob, became ill and lay dying and Mrs Ong was needed. For some inexplicable reason Eliza decided to take her eldest daughter to the old lady's bedside.

'I'd never seen anyone dead or dying, and I didn't want to go,' my mother told me. 'But Mother made me. I had to sit and watch Mrs Yaxley die. I thought it was cruel.'

'But why did she do it?' I asked. It seemed so unlike the loving, gentle grandmother I knew.

'She said it would be good for me. She said everyone had to learn about death and not be afraid when they saw it. But I was only 13 and I had nightmares about it for weeks.'

My grandmother was in no way morbid, or intentionally cruel, but she loved nursing and was dedicated to helping people wherever and whenever she could, and if sitting with them in their last hours eased and comforted them, then she would do just that – sit by their side, listen to their ramblings, soothe and minister until they needed her no longer. Her attitude was 'somebody's got to do it'. I believe she hoped that Doris would follow in her footsteps and make nursing her career.

The experience had a profound effect on my mother, if only to establish that the one thing she did not want to go into was nursing. Grandma never repeated the experiment, either with Doris or her sisters, but I had personal experience of her insistence on not being squeamish.

Billy Ashman, who delivered the papers, had been horribly disfigured in a fire; the skin of his face was stretched and shiny and he had no hair, not even eyebrows or eyelashes. His eyelids were scarred and his hands were so deformed that they were like inside out fists. He brought the papers on a bicycle, though how he managed to control it, I do not know. I am ashamed to say I was a little repulsed by him. One day, when we heard him ringing his bicycle bell at the garden gate, my grandmother, giving me some coins, said, 'Go and pay the paper boy.'

'I don't want to. He hasn't got any hands.'

'Of course he's got hands. Just you push the money under his thumb. Go on, he won't bite you. Give him the money and mind you smile at him.'

And so I did as I was told, bracing myself to push the pennies between the stump of his thumb and the ball of his hand and giving him a fixed little smile. Later, I asked my grandmother how he had come to be like that.

'When he was little, he and some other boys were playing with matches,' she said. 'They built a bonfire and when the flames were leaping up, they dare each other to jump over them. Billy slipped and fell into the fire. He nearly died. That's what can happen if you play with fire.' I was appalled. As a salutary lesson, it certainly worked. I could not forget it.

Slowly, so slowly as to be almost imperceptible at first, the tide of war began to turn. Reports of setbacks and retreats became fewer and reports of advances more frequent. On the eleventh hour of the eleventh day of the eleventh month of 1918, hostilities ceased and the country rejoiced. The church bells rang, bonfires were lit and in spite of the fact that the countryside was enveloped in fog and rain, everyone gathered laughing and singing to celebrate the end of all wars.

But the rejoicing was tinged with sadness. Twenty of Necton's young men had died, all of whom my grandparents knew well, including two Green boys, two Hubbard boys, Gerald Makins and the Squire's son, Captain Humfrey Mason. William Crockley, my grandmother's cousin, had been killed, and John Stibbon, Florence's husband, had his lungs ruined by poison gas and was never able to work again. Others had lost limbs or were blind or so shell-shocked they hardly knew which day it was, let alone the hour of that day. But many more were strong and healthy and fitter than they had ever been and they imagined they were coming back to a land fit for heroes.

While mourning those who had given their lives, Eliza and Walter were caught up in the gaiety. 'We went up to the village in the pony and trap,' Grandma told me. 'There was a good old party going on in the school and we had a rare old time, singing and dancing and drinking to victory. When it was time to go home, we found the pony where we had tethered it, lit up the lanterns and climbed in.

'Grandad was a bit unsteady and awkward and I could see I was goin' to hev a job with him. That poor little pony had stood all night while we enjoyed ourselves and then Grandad hadn't the patience to let it go home on its own. He giddy-upped suff'n fierce, so I say, "Here let me drive". He didn't want to let me, but he could see I meant it and in the end he let me take the reins. He always reckoned women were no good at driving, but I was just as good as he was, he just didn't want to admit it.' I smiled at this tale; it has its echoes today.

The Aftermath

DORIS WAS 13 when the war ended and had expected to leave school, but that year the school leaving age went up to 14 and she was granted a year's reprieve. She spent that time as a monitor, teaching the younger children and helping the new headmaster. Mr Stead, who had been at the school since before 1896, had retired and moved to Cambridge House and his place had been taken by Mr Clarke, who had lost a leg in France.

A great deal of discussion went on in that year as to what Doris should do when she left, which repeatedly came up against the same stumbling block – she did not want to leave school at all. Mr Clarke sowed the seeds of dissent when he told Walter and Eliza that he thought Doris should continue her education elsewhere, perhaps try for a scholarship to a teacher training college. But even with a scholarship, she would have to find her keep and there was no way her parents could manage it. Walter's frustration made him angry and he called Mr Clarke everything he could think of for filling his daughter's head with such 'high-falutin' squit'.

As far as he was concerned, at 14 you became a woman and were expected to begin earning a living, unless you belonged to the upper echelons of society who groomed their girls into young ladies fit only to become amusing and decorative until they met suitable young gentlemen and married them. She would have to leave school and begin work just as soon as she legally could and there were no two ways about it.

There were very few avenues open to country girls of working class families. In the city there were perhaps more, but even there, except for traditionally female occupations like housework and nursing, the girls were in competition with men returning from the armed forces. Domestic work it would have to be.

There were degrees of achievement even in this; the hierarchy of the servants' quarters was strictly adhered to, starting at the bottom with the scullion through kitchen-maid, chambermaid and parlourmaid up to ladies' maid. Or you could look after children and work your way up from nursery nurse to nanny. If you were lucky, you were one of many in the home of gentry, where your duties were clearly defined and you were well-fed, with specific periods of free time. It was better than being a maid-of-all work in a one-servant household where, besides pitiful wages, you had no time off.

All this was known to my mother, as it was known to every girl of her generation. It was a knowledge you grew up with; it had the inevitability of time passing. Your only hope was to find a good house where you were treated like an independent human being. That was all Doris asked, a certain amount of independence.

But her mother had other ideas. If Doris

was to be a servant, she might as well be a servant at home. The end of the war had coincided with the beginning of a 'flu epidemic, which was destined to carry off thousands of men, women and children all over Europe before it ended, and Eliza had never been so busy. She needed someone to look after the younger children while she worked. There was open rebellion at this suggestion. Although it made good sense to her mother, Doris hated the idea. A compromise was reached simply because an opportunity presented itself.

She went to work at the post office, which was at the other end of the village, near the church. 'I worked 12 hours a day, five and a half days a week,' she told me. 'But I was living at home, so I was on hand to look after the younger children and get them off to school if Mother got called out at night.'

In spite of the dreadful cost in human suffering the war had demanded and the added misery of the 'flu epidemic, there was a kind of euphoria. The ordinary labourer was earning 33s 7d, more than he had ever earned before. Cattlemen and horsemen earned 37s 10d and a shepherd 4d more than that. Expectations were high and at first it seemed they would be realised.

They were able to buy things they would never have dreamed of possessing before the war: gramophones, wireless sets and bicycles. Where before they had chosen their clothes for their practicability and hard-wearing qualities, now they studied fashion and were able to indulge it. Gone were the ladies' long restricting skirts, tight corsets and sturdy boots, they could afford the new shorter, looser skirts and fashionable shoes. The men, when they had fin-

ished their work, wore three-piece suits and well-ironed shirts and ties. They went out more, to the public houses, to the cinema and theatre. They had sickness insurance, widows' pensions and old-age pensions, now paid out at 65. With better husbandry and guaranteed prices, the farmers were doing well.

It was the landowners who were suffering. They had been forbidden to put up rents during the war and their tenants had been given security of tenure, so long as they obeyed the rules and regulations the government introduced. Much of the maintenance and repair of buildings, roads and drains for which they were responsible had been shelved for the duration of the war and was now urgently needed and becoming more costly by the day. The incentive to sell became almost overwhelming when the 1919 budget raised death duties.

Traditional country mansions came on the market almost on a daily basis, extolling the pleasures of hunting, shooting and fishing. Some of them were bought by businessmen who had amassed fortunes during the hostilities and wanted to buy large country properties as a kind of status symbol. They were prepared to pay dearly for the privilege and in the three years following the end of the war a quarter of the land in England changed hands. This disposal of land was worrying to the tenant farmers and many were either asked to quit by the new owners, who could then raise the rent to incoming tenants, or encouraged to buy their farms. Many of them did, borrowing the money to do so. After all, agriculture as a whole was doing well, and with guaranteed prices, what had they to lose?

But then the bubble burst. Inflation began to soar, the pound lost half its value and unemployment rose. Worst of all, the farmers' guaranteed prices were abandoned and the minimum wage for farm labourers was scrapped. The farmhand found himself earning 28 shillings a week when he needed at least 42 shillings to keep up with inflation. For four years the farms had survived with fewer men and many had improved their husbandry simply because they had had to. Mechanisation had increased, tractors were doing much of the work of horses and men; the jobs simply were not there any more. An exodus away from farming and country life began. Men from Norfolk went north to work in industry, 'into the sheres', just as Walter's brother, Charles, had done nearly 30 years before. With them went young Alfred.

He went to Lincolnshire and was lucky enough to find a job on a farm, living in with the farmer's family. But that was not what he really wanted; it was, after all, very little different from living at home and he might just as well be at Necton. So he came home, but not to farm work.

He had saved a little money from what he had been allowed to keep from his wages and bought a dilly cart, a kind of fish box on wheels, which he trundled to Holme Hale station at the crack of dawn every morning to load up with fresh fish. The fish was on its way from the east coast to the Midlands, but he had arranged to buy some of it. By breakfast time he was going from door to door in the village, selling it. He made a modest profit, enough to buy the next day's supply and, as his custom increased, he was able to buy more fish.

But his entrepreneurial efforts did not last. Housewives were finding even the cheapest fish beyond their means and he was struggling. His feet began to itch again and Eliza, who was always able to see and understand things about her family even before they knew about them themselves, realised he would soon be off again. She saw, in his restlessness and apparent discontent, echoes of her own early longings when she had fled from home. One day he would find what he wanted, the place where he wanted to stay, just as she had done. She loved Necton, would never have

Alfred as a young man.

Eliza in her working apron, taking time out to write a letter.

chatty letters, telling him all the goings-on in the family and village. She wrote exactly as she spoke; her letters were not elegant, nor well-punctuated, but eminently readable. While Alfred continued to receive her letters, he was not lost to them, however far he might travel.

Besides writing regularly to Alfred, she wrote to Doris and Gladys, her Aunt Sarah Crockley, and of course, Alice. Some of their letters had failed to cross the Atlantic during the war, but they had made up for it afterwards. Alice now had three children, Alice May, born in May 1915, John, born in April 1916 and Amy Victoria, born in October 1918, just as the war was drawing to a close. She and Frank were happy together and though she missed her family in England she had not regretted her decision to emigrate. She would have liked to come back for a visit, but it was not possible with a family to bring up, but perhaps one day, when the children were grown up, she would make the trip and then they could have a good old chin-wag.

David Ong, once hale and hearty, was getting on for 80 and after a series of strokes that left him completely helpless, did no more work. Eliza nursed him for a whole year, running backwards and forwards across the Drift whenever her mother-in-law summoned her and this besides her usual midwifery and nursing duties.

'We all loved him and he was fond of us, though he could be difficult at times,' my mother said when I asked her about him. 'He still thought of himself as the guv'nor. My father was expected to do as he was told, even at his age, though I don't think he did it without argument.'

I smiled at that. Grandad was one of the

dreamed of leaving it, probably because she loved Walter and his life was there; the two went together. But Alfred was different, he had to find his own way, his own anchor, and she had to let him go. She tried to talk Walter into understanding too, but I'm not sure she was altogether successful.

Within weeks Alfred was gone again and the next they heard of him, he was in Yorkshire and working in a public house. Eliza was pleased to hear from him and relieved that he appeared to be more settled. She sat down to write him one of her most argumentative men I have ever come across. I think he enjoyed a good fight just for the pleasure of besting someone and he would argue for the sake of it long after Grandma had convinced him he was wrong. Not that he was often wrong; he was as good a judge of man or beast as anyone alive and he had a love of truth and a confidence in his own opinions that made it difficult, even impossible, for him to remain quiet if he thought he was right.

But his father's illness meant that even more work devolved on him. Before he went to work he had to bait[19] his father's animals, draw water for his mother and make sure she had enough sticks and coal in the house, and the same again when he returned. It was this need to get every job done as fast as possible and get on with the next that contributed to the loss of the top of his thumb one frosty morning when he was operating a kibbler, a sort of liquidiser for animal feed. He still had it when I was young and I often watched him use it. He would stand over the machine with his feet apart and, taking the mangolds or other root crops from a heap at his feet, he would push them into the top of the hopper with his right hand while he turned the handle with the left. Too much haste, a moment's inattention and he would have turned the handle before his other hand had been fully withdrawn. On a cold day, with frost making steam of his breath and ice forming in sharp crystals on the mangolds, his hands would have been numb and not as quick as usual.

I never heard my grandfather swear, but I dare say he could if there were no children present to hear him and I imagine he might have done on this occasion. Pulling his ker-chief from his neck, he wound it round his bleeding thumb and went home for Eliza to wash and bandage it properly, then he went back to work. After all, what's half a thumb more or less?

After another stroke, David Ong died in the last week of April 1921. Eliza laid him out and his coffin was put on trestles in the front parlour so that relatives and friends could pay their respects. He was buried in the parched ground of Necton churchyard on the 3 May, mourned by his wife and family and a great many friends.

J. H. Wheals, carpenter-cum-builder-cum-undertaker of East Bradenham, submitted a bill on 30 April, even before the poor man had been laid to rest, for £8 3s 6d, which included the coffin, wadding for the shroud, the brass plate, 12 feet of oak planking taken to the churchyard for the grave and four bearers. It was paid in full on 12 May. In addition, the clergyman was paid 2s 6d and the sexton, Mr J. Fickling, 12s 6d.

David had changed his will in August 1920, some time after his first stroke when he was bedridden. The solicitor had attended him at the house and taken new instructions and his subsequent account mentioned the fact that he had attended Dr Allen who had said he was quite capable of understanding a will and quite able to make one. Whether this was standard practice or someone had suggested he was too ill to know what he was doing, I do not know.

He left Walter the smallholding, although his wife was to remain as tenant for life. He also set up a trust fund with his savings to benefit all the surviving children when their mother died. Walter and his

[19]feed

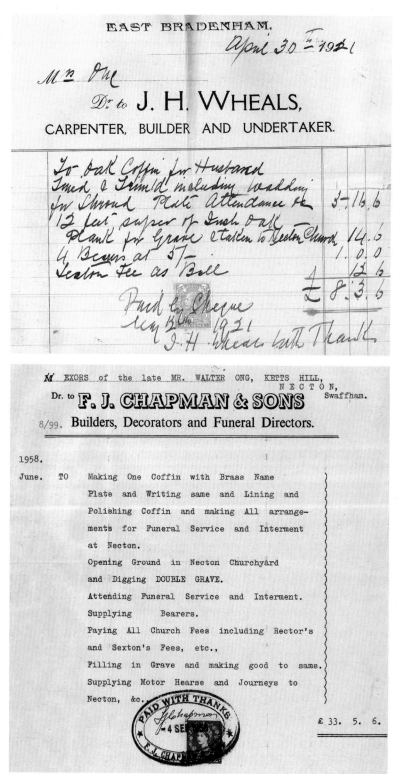

The undertaker's accounts for David and Walter Ong's funerals. Note the difference in cost after 37 years

mother were appointed trustees and Walter executor. It was not an arrangement that pleased Walter's sister, Elizabeth, who maintained the house and land should be sold and shared out with the rest when her mother died. Eliza was furious on Walter's behalf. He had worked so hard and always been there to help his parents, even when he had a young family of his own, and his father had recognised the fact.

It was one of the hottest and driest summers on record and the dykes dwindled to a trickle, the ponds in the corners of the fields dried up and the cattle cried out in thirst. Haysel and harvest were good that year, but it was only a respite. Worse depression lay ahead.

As the recession started to bite, farmers who had borrowed at high interest rates to buy their properties, found they could not afford the repayments. They survived on credit: they owed money to the blacksmith, the wheel-wright, the miller, the harnessmaker and the seedsman. As long as their credit held good and they could pay their men, they carried on, not knowing what else they could do. As soon as they failed to meet their wages bill, they went bankrupt and the farms changed hands again, for much lower prices. Large tracts of land, ploughed up during the war, reverted to gorse and bracken, running wild with rabbits. Those farmers who kept sheep fared best. The sale of the wool and surplus ewes brought in enough to replenish the stock and keep them going, just.

'They were still holding huge sheep auctions at Swaffham between the wars,' Grandma told me. 'Though now they were held on the Cricket Meadow and not in the market place like when Grandad was a lad. Sometimes 25,000 sheep would change hands in a single day. When they were sold, drovers pick 'em up a thousand at a time and drive them to the railhead or to their new farms, dropping the right number off at each stopping place. The drover had a boy helper and two or three dogs and he'd drive 'em along the lanes at a snail's pace.'

'You mean a sheep's pace,' I said.

'You're right there,' she said, with a smile at my joke. 'It was just as well there weren't many motor cars about in those days.'

Little had changed in the years since my grandfather had begun his life as a shepherd, but those few years were as nothing to the length of time men had been keeping sheep. It was a satisfying job for a countryman; its traditions remained unchanged and sheep, to a great extent, proved the saving of many a Norfolk farm from extinc-tion in the years between the wars. Walter, a key man on Mr Adcock's farm, enjoyed a certain amount of security, even if his wages were worth less than they had been owing to inflation.

Sarah Ong, getting old now, lived on alone while Walter struggled back and forth to work each day, trying to do the jobs of two men, and Eliza was kept busy looking after her own young family and being a Good Samaritan to half the village. The influenza epidemic, which had kept her more busy than she liked to be, was all but over but, now the men were back at home, the birth rate shot up. Bringing little people into the world was better than watching them die, though if the recession continued much longer she was afraid some might succumb to hunger.

The Second Midwives' Act had come into force at the end of the war, which made the Local Supervisory Authorities (LSAs) responsible for paying the doctors' and midwives' fees. These had to be recovered from the patients by the midwife and forwarded to the LSA for payment, but the poorer mothers-to-be could not afford them, so they did not bother to book a doctor and midwife in advance. When their labour pains began, they did as they always had and called on the services of Eliza, relying on her to send for a doctor if she thought it was necessary. If he was sent for as an emergency, then the county paid on receipt of a Medical Aid Form signed by the doctor.

It was about this time the decision was made that Doris should leave home. Although she was giving her mother almost all her pay, it was pitifully small and hardly enough to feed her. If Doris found a post where she could live in, it would relieve the financial situation and also the overcrowding in the cottage, which was bursting at the seams as the children grew up. Gladys would soon be leaving school and she could take her turn at looking after the younger children while Eliza was working.

How the subject came up, I do not know, but Eliza mentioned Doris to Dr Francis Allen, who had attended her father-in-law in his last illness. He may even have spoken to Doris himself during his visits to David, but however it came about, he said there was a vacancy for a parlourmaid at his home at Cockley Cley Hall and Doris could work for him.

Two weeks later, Doris packed her few clothes and personal possessions into the basket of her bicycle and cycled the 8 miles from Necton to Cockley Cley. She was accompanied by her father who cycled home again as soon as he saw her safely inside.

'I made her first cap and apron out of her christening robe,' my grandmother told me, as we sat side by side outside the cottage door, shelling peas that Aunt Norah had just picked from the vines. 'The skirt was very full and long and it had some fine tucking round the hem, so it was an easy job to make it into an apron and I made her two caps out of the sleeves. Her mistress say how neat and smart she look. I didn't let on how I'd done it though.'

Although she had to work hard, Doris did not dislike her job; she was learning how the well-to-do lived, how fashionable people dressed and behaved. She learned to appreciate nice furniture and good food and all the finer things of life, even if it was only

Doris posing in the apron and cap Eliza made for her from her christening robe. Eliza taught her granddaughter, Joan, how to make these aprons and Joan has made several for friends and family since.

at second hand. Being a parlourmaid, one of her duties was to serve afternoon tea, and she would lay up the tray with a cloth and with the china tea things set on it exactly so. To the end of her life, she always laid a tea tray properly, with a cloth and the milk in a jug and the jam in a basin with its own spoon. She would be horrified at the sight of a milk bottle on a tray and the jam in the pot in which it had been bought.

She had a half day off each week and once a month a whole Sunday off and then she cycled home, taking some little gift, usually of food, which Mrs Allen had given her. On Mothering Sunday, it was simnel cake, which all servant girls traditionally took home as a present for their mothers from their lady employers. The rest of the family gathered excitedly when she was expected home; they wanted to know what she had been up to and hear all the doings of the 'nobs', and also to see what she had brought to eat. When the time came to return, Walter would cycle all the way back with her. It did not matter how busy or how tired he was, he never allowed her to go back alone.

Then Walter himself became ill, complaining of severe pain in his abdomen and for once in his life he was unable to go to work. He was not one to fuss unnecessarily and he certainly looked ill, 'yeller as a paigle', my grandmother described him. In spite of his protests, she called the doctor. Gallstones were diagnosed and an immediate operation advised.

Walter would have none of it. No one was going to take a knife to him, however clever he thought he was. 'You kin't go ag'in nature,' he said. 'When my time come, I'll hatta go, and that's the hull on it.' Eliza pleaded in vain, pointing out that he ought to think of his family and his mother, who would all be in a pickle without him, but he was adamant. She was a good nurse, the very best, he told her, and she would look after him; he did not need to go to hospital.

Eliza delegated the housework and looking after the children to Gladys, cancelled all her midwifery bookings and devoted her whole time to her husband, snatching what sleep she could on a truckle bed at his side. But in spite of all her ministrations, he grew worse and it looked as though he really was going to die. She wrote to Alfred and Doris to prepare them for the worst.

'I woke up one night and found him wandering down the garden path in his nightshirt,' she told me. 'He were delirious and I had a fare job getting him back to bed. I took his hand and spoke real quiet. I was afraid he would light out at me, not knowing who I was or where he was, but I turn him round and lead him back in the end. It didn't do a ha'p'orth of good, that walk in the moonlight, his temperature shot up and he was raving with pain. In his more lucid moments both she and the doctor tried to persuade him to agree to the operation, but he was adamant. No doctor was going to open him up.

'Another night I woke up and he was lying there talking to someone at the foot of the bed, but there were no one there,' Grandma went on. 'I said, "Who are you talking to?" and he say, "Why, Polly. She want me to goo alonga her." Polly lived out Holme Hale way, near the Jolly Farmers, but we hadn't seen her for years. I told him I couldn't see anyone and he say, "That you kin. She be standin' right there." And he point to the end of the bed and say, "Git you along hoom, maw, it's late and you'll be missed." It seem she was asking him to go with her, but I couldn't see or hear anything. After a bit he dropped off to sleep.' She paused to let her words sink in and then added, almost as an afterthought. 'Next day I heard Polly had died that night.'

Why my grandfather should conjure that lady up, I had no idea and did not like to ask. She obviously wanted to take him with her wherever she was destined to go, but he was made of sterner stuff. He recovered, though whether he gave his wife any credit or put his recovery down to a benign fate, I don't know.

But it took a long time. Six weeks after he first fell ill, he had still not returned to work, and Mr Adcock, with no one to look after his animals, reluctantly dispensed with his services. He told Walter he was sorry, but he could not wait any longer and had hired a new man. It was not only the job Walter lost, but his home. It was a tied cottage and went with the job. Now the family were in desperate straits. Eliza had been unable to work while he was ill and though she went straight back to it, it was not the same as having a regular wage coming in. It was a terrible time. 'Sometimes we didn't know where our next meal was coming from,' she told me.

Aunt Gladys told my sister that Grandma had cooked her pet rabbit for dinner and she sat on the stairs and sobbed while the rest of the family were sucking the bones. I do not suppose, for a minute, the rabbit was killed without a great deal of soul-searching, but Gladys did not understand the necessity.

The Parish Relieving Officer visited them one day, though who suggested he should call, no one seemed to know. Certainly it was not Walter.

Eliza invited him in, hoping her husband would not be difficult, but even she was annoyed when the man began looking about him at their possessions as if weighing up what could be sold to help keep the family. 'That's a nice mantel clock,' he said, nodding towards it.

'It's a family heirloom,' Eliza said, watching their visitor opening cupboard doors, as if they might have a hidden stash

of gold there. All he saw were the usual pots and pans of a poor household, and Grandma's precious tea set.

'Grandad were as short as pie crust,' Grandma said. 'He said he wasn't a-gooin' to have some meddlin' busy-body poking about in his house. "You want to know what I ha' got," he said. "I'll show you." Then he turn his trouser pockets inside out to show they were empty. "Narthin', that's what."'

It hurt his pride and only the worried expression on Eliza's face, half hope, half fear of what he would do or say next, made him swallow it and accept the 2 shilling piece which was finally offered. He looked down at the coin lying on the table where the man had placed it, but somehow he could not bring himself to pick it up.

'Do you have a bicycle?' the man asked suddenly, taking Walter by surprise. His questions had been pretty searching before he had parted with the largesse, so why did it make a difference if he had a bicycle? Surely he was not going to suggest he sell that to buy food?

'Yes,' he answered slowly.

'Does it have a puncture outfit?'

'Yes.' By now, even Eliza was puzzled.

'My bicycle has a puncture, do you think you could ask your boy to repair it for me?'

A slow smile spread itself across Walter's face. He picked up the florin and handed it back. 'Here, tek this,' he said. 'Buy yarself a puncture outfit.'

Pride had triumphed, but it left them worse off than before. They could expect no help from that quarter now and they only had a week to get out of the cottage.

Who suggested the solution, I do not know, but it seemed the only thing they could do. They moved, lock, stock and barrel, across the Drift to live with Sarah.

It needed a tremendous adjustment on everyone's part, not least Eliza's. Her mother-in-law had never been exactly fond of her and two women in one small cottage was bound to cause friction. And small it was. There were just two bedrooms for three adults and five children between the ages of fourteen and six. They resolved it by buying a wooden hut, which was erected end on to the cottage's back door

and furnished with their own bedroom furniture, leaving Sarah in possession of the biggest of the two upstairs bedrooms and the children to share the other. It was an almost impossible squeeze. But at least Sarah could keep an eye on the children when Eliza was called out.

Mr and Mrs Bunyan and their two children moved into the cottage across the Drift. If Walter felt any resentment about that he would not have said so. It was simply the way things were.

A Terrible Time

THE MOVE ACROSS the Drift coincided with Gladys's time to leave school and she joined my mother at Cockley Cley Hall as a chambermaid, leaving Arthur, the twins and Audrey at home. Sarah invested in a few sheep, which Walter kept on the meadow beside the orchard. They had a pig and a cow and grew their own vegetables, and the 12-year

Walter with his sheep.

old Arthur did what he could to help. They survived with their pride intact.

Walter was offered work by Mr Eustace Makins, who farmed Wood Farm on the road to Little Fransham, not far from where Eliza's grandparents had had their brickworks. He walked across the fields to his work, which was quicker than taking his bicycle round by the road, and he did a full day there before returning home. Eliza gave a huge sigh of relief and set herself the task of living in contentment with her mother-in-law.

In spite of the hard times, there were little high spots of enjoyment. On Good Friday there was a tea party for which everyone was charged sixpence. 'We had to go to chapel first,' I was told by Dolly Bell, who was one of the children. 'But there was always a good turn out. There was a huge teapot and paste and jam sandwiches and slab cake, just as there was for the Sunday School outing. We played postman's knock and twirling the plate and sticking the tail on the donkey. There was a party at Christmas too. The food was the same only you got a mince pie as well.'

The annual Sunday School outing, curtailed because of the war, was revived. Now that Alfred, Doris and Gladys were at work, it was Eliza's younger children who went. They were supervised on these outings by the Sunday School teachers and those mothers who had volunteered their services, and that included Eliza.

Sometimes they were taken to Hunstanton. They played on the beach and paddled in the sea and each was given an ice cream. Their packed tea was eaten on the Green, washed down with lemonade made with bright yellow crystals before they climbed back into the cart and returned home, tired but very happy. It was the highlight of their year and they talked about it for weeks afterwards, recounting what they had seen and done and impatiently looking forward to the following year, which seemed an eternity away.

On another occasion, when they went to Castle Acre, Sarah decided to go too, but she became bored and irritable with the noise of the children and decided to go home. Castle Acre is a good five miles from Necton, but she set off undeterred, striding along the lanes in her black buttoned boots, long skirt and black cape. The returning wagon caught up with her before she had gone very far and she graciously agreed to ride the rest of the way.

On Saturdays the women would go shopping in Swaffham using what was laughingly called a 'bus' service. Mr Cousins had bought himself a lorry when

The Sunday school outing to Castle Acre, c.1922 (most of the children are Eliza's 'babies'). Back row left to right: Mrs Hudson holding daughter Joyce, Mrs Thrower, Mrs Symonds, Mrs Gilding, Mr Gilding, Mr Clark, Mrs Clark (née Mary Thrower), Eliza Ong, Mrs Claxton, Sarah Ong, Mrs Ellen Yaxley (who was midwife to Eliza) holding daughter Ruby. Second row, seated: Mrs Lydia Yaxley, Hilda Powley, Edith Johnson, Maud Gage, Ada Cullen, Harriet Clark. Third row, kneeling: Violet Thrower, Edna Lincoln, Daisy Powley, Herbert Symonds, Stanley Symonds, Jimmy Cullen, Norah Ong, Mr Anderson, Sunday school teacher, Leslie Hudson, Ernest Yaxley, Arthur Ong, Herbert Lincoln, Oswald Powley. Seated in the foreground: Roy Yaxley, Elsie Lincoln, Gladys Yaxley (looking back), Dolly Powley (peeping from behind her), Irene Goff, Roy Claxton, Doris Thrower, Vera Claxton, Audrey Ong, Emma Ong, Edna Claxton, Mabel Thrower, Ethel Yaxley.

he came out of the army and set himself up as a haulage contractor, carrying sugar beet. Every Saturday lunch time, he cleaned the lorry out, put two forms down each side and a tarpaulin over the top and advertised it as a passenger service to take people to Swaffham. 'He made steps up into the back with a stepladder,' Dolly Bell told me. 'He charged sixpence for the return fare and he always had plenty of takers. It was better than walking or cycling, if you had shopping to carry.'

It was also a wonderful gossip shop. Sitting close together in the gloomy confines of the lorry, someone would say, 'I hear so and so's expectin' ag'in and her last nobbut a year old.' Or, 'D'yer hear so and so's youngest is getting wed and not afore time, if yer ask me.' Or, 'That a new hat, Maud? I hin't seen it afore.' 'No, well I never notice it.' And again. 'What are you plannin' on making with that bit o' muslin, Eliza?'

In 1923, the farms were struck by a foot and mouth epidemic and hundreds of cows had to be shot. Their carcasses could not be taken off the farms and had to be burned on the spot. Hardened men stood by with tears running down their faces as the smoke and stench of the huge funeral pyres filled the air. The farmers, now in desperate straits, offered their employees 24s 9d for a 54-hour week with a reduction for 'wet time', which would have reduced their wages even more.

The Agricultural Workers' Trade Union called a strike and the dispute affected all the eastern counties. The farmers could not work the land without the men and a settlement was finally reached providing a guaranteed week of 50 hours for 25 shillings and further hours up to 54 were to be paid at the rate of sixpence an hour. Although this was better than nothing, the men still had no paid holidays – the only paid time off they had was Christmas Day and Good Friday.

When it was Arthur's turn to leave school, he had little chance or even inclination to go into agriculture. Instead he went to work as a back'us boy at Weasenham Hall for Mr Somerset de Chair, author and Member of Parliament, where Hilda Powley was also in service. Now there were only the twins and Audrey living at home, though that did not mean Eliza's workload was any less. People were still falling sick and dying and babies were still being born and, because there was so much poverty, the women could not afford to call in the doctor, nor even the official midwife, who was obliged to collect the proscribed fee for her services.

Sometimes Eliza would take beef tea or chicken broth to her patients, if she knew they could not afford it themselves. Whenever I have spoken to any of the older members of the village community, I have been told how much she did and how competent and cheerful she always was. 'But if she said the doctor ought to come, then we sent for him and worrited how we were going to pay for him afterwards,' I was told.

In October 1925, the 17-year-old Cecil Powley became ill and Eliza, being sent for, realised that this was no ordinary bout of 'flu and advised Maud to call the doctor. The result was that Cecil was rushed to Swaffham hospital where meningitis was diagnosed. He lingered for two weeks and every day Eliza harnessed the pony and trap and took Maud to visit her son. (Now she had got her way about driving, Walter reluctantly allowed her to take the trap out on her own.) When Cecil died on 13 October, the whole of Ivy Todd was shocked and frightened. Could it happen to anyone else? How could they prevent it? Fortunately it was an isolated case, but my grandmother mourned the loss with her friend and did all she could to support her in her bereavement, looking after the others in the family and helping with the funeral tea. Not that she told me this herself; I heard it from Maud's daughter, Dolly.

'She came up when young Norman had pneumonia, too,' she told me. 'He was only five and my mother was very frightened because he was so ill and she thought we were going to lose him like we had Cecil, but Granny Ong sat with him, then she said, "The crisis has passed and he's sleeping peacefully. He'll be all right now."'

In 1926, in the middle of the worst depression anyone could remember, yet another midwives' act decreed that uncertified midwives, like Eliza, could not attend a birth as a midwife except in an emergency and then they must satisfy the authorities that 'attention was given in a case of sudden or urgent necessity'. This was a way out for the unqualified practitioners because they simply claimed the birth had been an emergency and the 'proper' nurse could not get there in time. 'Was I supposed to stand by and let the poor woman die?' Eliza demanded. The general practitioner often connived in this, especially when he knew the midwife in question was competent and would not fail to call him when necessary. Many an infant was reported as 'born before arrival'.

Dr Thorpe, Dr Moss and Dr Townend were all happy to work with Eliza. If they knew she had been booked for a confinement they did not worry too much if they were delayed in getting to it themselves. 'I know if Mrs Ong is on the case, I'm all right,' Dr Townend said more than once.

It was about that time that Doris came home to tell them that Dr Allen was going to sell Cockley Cley Hall. 'He called us all together to tell us,' she told her parents. 'He said he wasn't sure how many of us would be kept on by the new owner and if we found ourselves new jobs, he'd give us all good characters.'

Good jobs were very difficult to come by and this was a blow, but Doris told them Dr Allen had taken her to one side and said he was pleased with her work and thought she deserved something better. He had been in touch with a consultant friend in London who needed a receptionist and he was prepared to recommend her for the post.

'London?' queried Walter. 'I in't hevin' you go all that way.'

'Why not?' Doris demanded. Like her brother, Alfred, she wanted to open up her horizons and this seemed a wonderful opportunity. 'I'll be bettering myself. And the pay is twice what I'd get hereabouts.'

'And what would you be gettin' up to in London, eh?' her father demanded. As far as he was concerned, the capital was a million miles away and a wicked place to boot. 'All manner of tomfoolery, I'll be bound.'

'Pa don't be silly. I won't get up to anything, and it's a better job than I'll ever get round here.'

'And who are you calling silly, eh? I'm yar father, girl, and don't you forget it. Yar not so big I can't give yer a clip if I've a mind to.'

'What's he do, this consultant?' Eliza asked, before matters got out of hand and things were said that could not be unsaid.

'He's an eye specialist and his name's Sir John Tweedie,' Doris answered. 'His partner's Mr Philips and he specialises in tropical diseases.'

'Tropical diseases in London?' Walter queried. He was unhappy and suspicious, and though Eliza could see his point of view, she was not going to oppose her daughter. Doris was every bit as stubborn as her father and had the same urge to do something different as Alfred. She could hardly blame either of them.

'Why not?' Doris insisted. 'It's in Harley street, it's where all the top doctors live. I'll be meeting all the best people. They pay hundreds of pounds for their consultations.'

'Are you really set on going?' Eliza asked her.

'Yes, Mum.'

Eliza sighed. 'Then there's no more to be said. But just make sure you write reg'lar and come home when you can.'

And so Doris went to Harley Street. 'I had to answer the door and show the patients into the waiting room,' she told me. 'It wasn't like an ordinary doctor's waiting room, it was more like a drawing room. And I had to serve them tea and tell Sir John they were there, and then show them into the surgery. I had a lovely uniform and proper time off and I loved living in London.'

Her mother's letters kept her in touch with what was happening in Necton, and occasionally she would be given a weekend

Doris just before her wedding, 1929.

off and returned home by train, to be met at the station by her father with the pony and trap. She was 21 years old and according to Audrey, her youngest sister, then 11, she was very grown up and sophisticated. 'She had nice clothes and her hair was cut and waved and I thought she was wonderful,' my aunt told me. 'When she came home, I would follow her about like a little dog. I wanted to be just like her when I grew up.'

Doris was at home one Sunday in August when all but the heaviest sleepers and those already about their business were awakened at five am by a deep rumbling that many at first took to be thunder.

But it soon became apparent that it was more than that. Beds shook, ornaments rattled, pictures fell off the walls and the dogs began to bark.

At the time Eliza was in another house in the village, helping a doctor do an appendectomy on a small child on a window sill. 'Whatever was that?' she asked, being careful not to let the light she was holding waver. He looked up momentarily from what he was doing, but quickly returned to his task as a second rumble shook the little cottage. It was not until the next day, when the child was safely tucked up in bed,

Norah with the pony and trap.

The twins, Emma (left) and Norah, early 1930s.

having successfully survived the operation, that they learned that it had been an earthquake. My grandmother said it was all in a day's – or a night's – work and she was thankful it had not had any adverse effect on their patient.

The twins left school that year. Eliza, as usual, looked about for suitable posts for them and, when the opportunity arose at one of the Friendship Club meetings, she mentioned the matter to Miss Mason. 'Well, I could take one of them,' she said, 'but not both, I am afraid.' So Emma started work at the Hall as a kitchenmaid; later she became a cook.

Eliza, hearing that there was a vacancy at Sandringham House, applied on Norah's behalf. My aunt was granted an interview with whoever was responsible for hiring the indoor servants but she was turned down on the grounds that she was too short. 'All the servants hatta be the same height when they line up,' she told me. 'It didn't matter if you were likely to be good at the job.'

I do not think my aunt would have been happy with the job. She hated being indoors; her days were spent outside, among the animals. She became the 'daughter at home' and helped on the smallholding, taking casual jobs on the land when and where they became available. I remember asking her why she had not married, which was very presumptuous of me, but she simply smiled and said, 'I'm waiting for Mr Right to come along.' She was strong and wiry, and there were few jobs on the land she could not do. In many ways my grandfather treated her like another son and they were very close.

Sandringham was near enough to Necton for the doings of the Royal family to be local gossip and Grandma always took a keen interest in them. Queen Mary, particularly, was well-known in Swaffham because of a particular antique shop she patronised. It was owned by a man called Fountain Winter, who had hung an ugly iron man-trap over the door on the day his first grandson was born and the locals always referred to it as 'Winter's Little Nipper'. The shop was next to the rates office and shared the same front door and entrance passage.

Grandma was in the rates office one day when she heard a commotion outside and the sound of cheering, and being curious, hurried out to see what was going on. She quite literally bumped into Queen Mary. Because the passage was narrow and the Queen's entourage had naturally stood aside to let her enter first, Her Majesty took the full force of Grandma's weight, slight though it was, and she recoiled under the impact.

'She was so haughty,' Grandma said. 'She step back and look down her nose at me and say. "Who is this person?" as if I'd no right to be alive, let alone git in her way.'

I was completely overawed by this tale and said, 'Whatever did you do?'

'I said "Sorry, ma'am", dropped a quick curtsey and went back into the rates office 'til she'd gone. I was trembling all over, but then I put it to myself, she's only a woman, after all, and I'm as good as she is, so I pull myself together and thought no more on it.' All the same it was a story she always told with relish.

Necton was one of the favourite meets of the West Norfolk Hunt and had been since 1696 when the Squire Mason of those times established a pack of foxhounds at the Hall. There was a good pheasant shoot each year too, and the local men would earn a few shillings extra as beaters. 'Sport they call it,' my grandfather said. 'Up goo seven and six, bang goo tuppence and down come half a crown.'

I did not realise he was repeating a maxim that was common at the time and asked my grandmother to explain. 'It cost seven and six to rear the bird,' she told me, 'the cartridge cost tuppence and then all you can get for the bird when you sell it is half a crown. Not very profitable, is it?'

Necton Hall was famous for its red poll cattle and its butter, which was made twice a week in one pound blocks, with 'Necton Butter' stamped on the top. These were taken to Swaffham market in a huge box lined with lead shelves and filled with ice, a kind of early refrigerated container. It found a ready market, but any unsold surplus was offered to the villagers, along with the skimmed milk, a by-product and often the only milk the poorer households could afford.

Mr Mason, besides being a founder of the Red Poll Society, was a magistrate, an alderman, a governor of Swaffham Grammar School and of Necton village school. To nearly all, he was either their landlord or their employer's landlord and the men would touch their caps or forelocks to him, out of respect, not because they were afraid of him. He was astute and fair to all and not above sending for my grandmother if someone in the household needed nursing.

When he died in October 1927, his obituary in the local papers was a long one and the report of his funeral at Necton church listed hundreds of mourners, from the highest to the lowest. Those who could not get into the church, lined the road outside along with the local schoolchildren, all in their Sunday best, and stood silently as the cortège went by.

The estate was inherited by Mr Mason's son who lived in Yorkshire, but he never took up residence in Necton and the hall was sold to a Mr Bond of Lowestoft. It was the end of an era as far as the villagers were concerned. They never had another squire.

There was a hard winter that year and the thaw in January 1928 brought floods to many parts of the country. The pit was brimming and the little river at the end of Ivy Todd flooded Leather Bottle Lane. The Rump family, who lived down there, were marooned in their home. They stood at their garden gate on one side of the water and caught the food thrown to them by the villagers from the other side, until the water subsided far enough for them to wade out and do their shopping.

Doris had news too. She had changed her job and was now a nanny for Judge Wrangham at Dawson Place. 'I looked after the children,' she told me. 'I gave them their meals and took them out for walks and made sure they behaved themselves.' But that job did not last long because that same year my mother met and fell in love with the handsome guardsman who was to become my father. Adrian Leendert VanderVlies was of Dutch extraction, though he had been born in South Africa and had become a naturalised British citizen. He was in the Third Battalion of the Grenadier Guards and was stationed at Caterham. I think they met in the park when Doris was taking her charges for a walk.

She took him home on one of her weekends off and my grandfather took an immediate dislike to him. It was not anything he did or said, simply that he was a 'furriner' and in the regular army, both good reasons for opposing a marriage between the two.

As usual Eliza kept her own counsel and tried to mitigate her husband's gruff manner by making the newcomer welcome, but the visit was not a success. Walter might have hoped the romance would die a natural death, but it proved not to be the case because in the early summer of 1929, Doris wrote and told them that on 9 July she was going to marry Adrian at Thurrock where his parents lived.

Eliza was very disappointed that her daughter would not be marrying from home, but she could see Doris's point of view. Walter had set his mind against the match and the occasion would not be the happy one it should have been, and though she wanted very much to attend, Eliza dare not oppose her husband. Doris married without any of her family being present. As far as Walter was concerned, she had made her bed, she must lie in it.

Adrian's enlistment was for three years with the colours and nine years on the reserve, and now the three years was up, he was a civilian again. His father was an engineer and dredgerman and he was going out to Singapore to work on the new dry dock and there was a job for Adrian too if he wanted it.

On 10 August 1929, they sailed on the *SS Katori Maru* for Singapore. I do not know if my mother went home again before she left, but I am quite sure that as far as Eliza was concerned it was worse than her parting from Alice, made even more heartbreaking because Walter would not allow her to talk about her daughter. Pictures of her were removed from the walls and there is not a single photograph of her wedding in existence.

When Audrey, the youngest of Walter and Eliza's brood, approached her 14th birthday that summer, the usual discussions took place about what she should do. Mr Clarke had unfortunately died but his wife had taken over as headmistress and she was very disappointed that Audrey was not going to continue her education. She was a very bright girl and had won a scholarship when she was 11, but Walter had put his foot down about letting her go to Swaffham Grammar School. 'Scholarships are all verra well,' he had said when Audrey came home from school with the exciting news. 'But that in't the end on it, is it? You hatta get there and there's yar uniform to find.'

'We'd manage it somehow,' Eliza had said.

'Mayhap, but none of the others could go and it i'n't fair to them to mek a favourite of her. 'sides, she'll be getting above herself.'

He would not be budged and Audrey had continued at the village school. When it was time for her to leave, Mrs Clarke went to see Walter and Eliza and pointed out that there were many more opportunities for girls then than there had been when Doris had left school and Audrey ought to train for a proper career. Just because one child did not go on to further education, there was no reason to deprive another.

Walter's fragile temper over anything to do with education boiled over. 'My children are not deprived,' he shouted. 'None on 'em. They've been fed and clothed and sent to school, and there aren't none on 'em without a job and there's plenty can't say that.'

He was right in a way. Unemployment was a cross many had to bear, mature adults as well as school leavers, and as far as he was concerned, the sooner she found employment the better. I think from what she told me, my aunt would have liked to do something more interesting than going into service as all her sisters had done, but she knew better than to argue with her father when his temper was up and I don't think she held it against him.

As always my grandmother, while bowing to the inevitable as far as her daughter going into service was concerned, was determined that she would go to the best employer that could be managed, where she would learn a bit more than how to skivvy. Audrey went to work in the Earl of Albemarle's household at Eccles Hall. The estate covered a vast acreage at Quidenham and Eccles Road, two adjacent villages between Thetford and Attleborough, near enough for her to come home when she had a day off. How Eliza knew there was a vacancy I do not know, but like many things in those days, it was probably word of mouth.

Now that six of the seven children were 'off their hands' as they called it, Walter and Eliza were left with only Norah and old Sarah, who was becoming more and more difficult. Walter, at 58, was as busy as ever and Eliza was in constant demand and, I think, glad to get out of the house and do something she enjoyed, helping other people.

The recession, which had eased a little in the preceding year or two, deepened again. The stock market crashed and the fall in farmers' income was so severe that no reduction in costs or change in the way things were done or the type of crops they grew, could save thousands from bankrupt-

Mr Nelson standing in the doorway of his butcher's shop. The man by the delivery van is Ralph Green.

cy. Several Necton farms stood empty for years. Walter had the smallholding to supplement his income, so they managed better than most, but many of the villagers were in dire straits and my grandmother helped where she could, a little beef tea or chicken broth for her patients, a pie or cake for a large family, milk or eggs for the nursing mothers. 'If they want meat for the family,' my grandmother told me, 'they hatta go to the butcher's just before closing time on a Saturday night, when they get stewing beef at fourpence a pound, if'n it hadn't all been sold during the day.'

The women provided themselves and their children with clothes from what were called 'rummage sales' – jumble sales they are called today – often unpicking the garments and remaking them for a better fit. In big families, hand-me-downs were the order of the day and only the eldest and those old enough to go to work and earn a few shillings for themselves, had the

Mr Powley with four of his daughters outside their home (before they moved to Chapel Lane). Dolly, on the left, is wearing the velvet dress Eliza gave her.

privilege of 'new clothes'. Dolly Bell told me that my Aunt Audrey, three years older than she was, had a green velvet dress which she coveted. When Audrey grew out of it, Eliza gave it to Dolly and she was as thrilled as if it had been spanking new.

In the 1930s, families paid a penny or perhaps twopence a week to the Hospital Savings Association to cover a stay in hospital and another twopence went to the District Nursing Association, which meant the patient paid only 30 shillings instead of £2 10s. for midwifery. But many could not afford even that and they went on as before, sending for Eliza.

Mr Stead, one-time headteacher, was one of her patients. Although he had retired, he had remained in the village and Grandma was with him when he died. Later the house was occupied by Mr and Mrs Makins. When Mrs Makins became ill, Grandma was sent for.

'Mrs Makins loved a drop of whisky,' my mother told me, 'but her husband wouldn't let her have it. He said it was bad for her. Mother used to collect empty bottles until she had enough on the returns to buy a little bottle of whisky, which she smuggled in to the old lady. She would have a teaspoonful at a time, no more.' Grandma knew the old lady was dying and was of the opinion that 'a little drop of what you fancy does you good', a maxim with which the doctor agreed or she would not have done it.

I can't believe that Mr Makins did not know what was happening, he would surely have smelled drink on his wife's breath, even if he saw no evidence of the bottle. If he did, he did not hold it against the nurse because when he became ill himself in 1942, he would have no one to minister to him but Mrs Ong.

Eliza and Vi and Maud were still the best of friends and they would go to the Friendship Club together or snatch a few moments in one another's houses to have a chinwag and smoke a Woodbine. Grandma enjoyed a cigarette in spite of Grandad's disapproval. 'If the Lord ha' meant us to smoke, he'd ha' made us with chim'leys,' I often heard him say.

From time to time Walter and Eliza heard from Alfred, who was now working at the Hop Grove Hotel in Rufforth and had met the woman he intended to marry. Their wedding was set for 7 June 1930. Rachel, naturally, wanted to be married from her own home, as was customary, and Walter, who never travelled anywhere that could not be reached in an hour with the pony and trap, decided Yorkshire was too far to go. Once again, Eliza was thwarted, but Arthur went to be his brother's best man.

Births, Marriages and Deaths

WHEN HIS SON, Philip, was born on 14 May 1931, Alfred was overjoyed and sat down to write to his parents. But, as usual, sitting still was almost impossible for him. He went to see his great pal, Josh, to wet the baby's head and it was while he was talking to him, he thought of the idea. 'Why don't I go home and tell them? I could be there quicker than a letter.'

'By train, you mean?'

'No, on my bike.'

'It's 200 miles each way man, and that old bike o' yours is fit only for the scrap heap. You must be mad.'

'I like a challenge. Why not come with me?'

'Me? My bike's worse'n yours.'

'You'll see Norah.'

That was the deciding factor apparently. Josh had met Norah when she had come to Rufforth to stay with her brother for a few days and Josh had taken a shine to her. 'OK, but what about Rachel?'

'She's being well looked after and she won't mind.'

I have no idea whether Aunt Rachel minded or not, but the next day the two men set out very early. Alfred's cycle had no saddle and he had tied a bit of cloth over

Rachel, Alfred's wife, wearing Walter's hat and coat to feed the chickens, 1931.

the top of the frame to pad it a bit, and Josh's had only one pedal and it was hard work pedalling with only one foot. When the backside of one became sore and the leg of the other stiff, they changed machines, so that they could each torture another part of their anatomy.

I do not know how long they took over the journey, but I do not think they stopped for more than an hour or two to rest at intervals along the way. But they made it, arriving at Black Drift exhausted but elated. The news of Philip's arrival was imparted to an astonished Walter and Eliza and was toasted with a drop of the hard stuff. They stayed overnight, ate a hearty breakfast and then cycled back in the same way. It had been a disappointing trip as far as Josh was concerned; he had proposed to Norah and been turned down and he never tried again.

The news from Singapore took a little longer to arrive. I had been born on 8 May, just six days before Philip, and had been named Mary Elizabeth. Eliza was pleased that the names chosen for me reflected her own and she took it as a sign that all was well between her and her daughter.

In August 1931, Sarah Ong died, aged 90. Her funeral, which was well-attended, cost £15 10s, almost double that of David's funeral just over 10 years before. The coffin was £8, the bearers were paid £1 and burial fees were 12s 6d. Motor cars and telegrams were £1 17s 6d and having Sarah's name added to David's on the gravestone was £4.

Afterwards, their solicitor had the task of distributing the trust fund to the beneficiaries. His hand-written account shows that David Ong's trust fund, invested in war inscribed stock, stood at £745 plus the proceeds from selling furniture and effects, which brought the amount up to £761 10s 1d. After paying Doctor Moss, the funeral

The solicitor's account of David Ong's trust fund.

expenses, the commission for cashing in the war stock, selling and carting the furniture plus his own fees, there was £731 10s. 5d. left to be distributed.

Walter's sister, Hannah, was slow in returning the form the solicitor sent her and he had to write more than once to remind her. A letter he wrote to Walter comes over as rather peevish, or perhaps the poor man was simply frustrated.

She says she has been away for three weeks and found my letter on her return. And also that if my letter had been written to her at Leytonstone, it would have been forwarded. As a matter of fact the first letter with the account and form of receipt which she now returns was sent to Leytonstone and therefore she must have received it.

I am writing today with cheques to Mrs Stibbon, Mr Arthur Ong and Mrs Akers for £146 6s 1d. I am sending you herewith your cheque for £143 6s 1d, being the amount of your share after deducting £3 as shown in the account.

[The £3 was apparently cash Sarah had in the house when she died. Walter, as always, had been scrupulously honest in declaring it.] In a postscript, the solicitor added: The Bank will allow 23 shillings interest on the money and if you agree, I think this should be paid to me for extra correspondence etc in consequence of Mrs Akers' delay. I have filled up a cheque for 23 shillings and if you sign it and return it I shall be obliged.

In those days £731 was a fair amount and David must have been either very careful or an exceptionally good husbandman to have been able to save in those early years before the World War I, when Walter was dashing about trying to hold down a job, look after his family and help his father at the same time. No doubt the money came in very handy at that time of rising unemployment and hard times.

My brother, John, was born in August the following year and in 1934 our parents brought us back to England. One of the first things my mother did on her return was to take us to Necton. Grandma was delighted to see us and Grandad, who rarely showed any kind of emotion, accepted his daughter back into the fold and even managed to be polite to Adrian.

My sister, Ann, was born in April 1936, which was also the year George V died, the year of the Jarrow Hunger March and the year of the abdication, which filled the newspapers, but in Necton, there were other important things happening. Mr Somerset de Chair bought Necton Hall and my Uncle Arthur was offered the job of gardener-handyman on the estate, which had a cottage to go with it, enabling him to

Walter with granddaughter Angela, 1937.

The Good Woman Bowls Club, 1930s. Gordon Hubbard's son, Brian, had been rehearsed to present the bouquet to Mrs Somerset de Chair, but when the time came, he forgot everything and threw it at her before running away. Back row, left to right: Jack Hubbard, Arthur Ong, Basil Hubbard, Jack Bell, Ralph Green, Albert Blomefield, J. Fickling, Ted Bell, Ben Brown, (the next two are unidentified). Second row: Albert Farrow, Billy Larwood (dairy farmer, only just visible), Jimmy Heyhoe, Mr Tuffins, Jack Goodings (butcher), Gordon Hubbard holding the trophy; (the next three are unidentified). Seated: Mr and Mrs Somerset de Chair, owners of Necton Hall.

marry his childhood sweetheart, Hilda Powley. At the same time Hilda's sister, Daisy, married Stanley Frost, making it the only double wedding to be held in the village in living memory. The reception was held at the Three Tuns.

In the same year Audrey, just 21 years old, married Walter Took, known to everyone as Dick, whom she had met at Eccles Hall where he was a pigman. Unlike Adrian, he was approved of by Walter. They were married at Necton and afterwards Eliza put on a wedding breakfast at the smallholding and the newly-married couple posed outside the door for pho-

tographs. After the ceremony they lived on the Albemarle estate and their daughter, Angela, was born there in 1938. My aunt had the local district nurse for the delivery, but Grandma was there next day to see that all was well and to help with the new baby.

At a time when more and more workers were enjoying a week's paid holiday at the seaside, my mother took us to Necton. But that did not mean we never saw the sea. One day every summer I would come down to breakfast to find my grandmother making sandwiches and I knew we were going to have our annual treat to Wells-

next-the-Sea. My brother and perhaps our cousin, Philip, would already be gulping down their breakfast and I would hurriedly join them, while Grandma filled a flask with tea and two bottles with lemonade. Afterwards I fetched my swimsuit and a towel, while the boys went off to the middle shed to find the buckets and spades, which came out every year. By the time everything was ready, Mr Hubbard was at the gate.

Gordon Hubbard was the landlord of the Good Woman, the only public house of that name in the country, but he was also the owner of one of the few motor cars in Necton and he would hire himself and his car out on an hourly or daily basis, meeting people from trains, taking them to the hospital or, as in our case, out for a day. We were three very excited children as we piled our picnic basket, buckets and spades and car rug into the boot and scrambled inside, chattering like a trio of magpies.

On one occasion, we did not go directly to the coast, but stopped at a house in Fakenham, where we were joined by the elderly lady who lived there. She was, our grandmother told us as we set off again,

Lily Hubbard, Gordon Hubbard's daughter, with her father's car.

Sarah Crockley, Eliza's aunt.

with the boat would remember to come and fetch us back. He did, of course, and we returned to have our picnic on a bench on the sea front. At teatime Mr Hubbard returned from wherever he had spent his day and we went back to Necton, taking Great Auntie home on the way.

The following day my grandmother, or my mother if she was there, would boil the cockles and we sat outside to separate them from their shells, watched closely by the cat, who stretched out a paw every now and again to try and hook one of the shelled cockles out of the bowl. His paw was gently slapped by my grandmother and he retreated, but not very far, knowing he would eventually be rewarded. The empty shells were scattered along the garden path, to be mixed by tramping feet with the cinders, which were always thrown down there when the fire was cleaned out. They made a dry, well-drained surface that crunched nicely underfoot and you could always hear someone coming up the garden path when you were indoors. That evening we had cockles in vinegar with bread and butter for our tea and they were delicious.

We did not think anything would ever change. There were births, marriages and deaths, of course, and my grandmother knew as much as anyone about those, but they hardly impinged on our lives. We knew all our grandmother's callers and they knew us.

Mr Goodings, the butcher, called twice a week and whenever he saw any of us children he would cut off a lump of raw suet and give it to us, wiping his bloodied butcher's knife on a cloth before cutting it. We would walk up the path nibbling. I

her Aunt Sarah and therefore our great-great-aunt, but that was far too many greats to cope with and we always called her Great Auntie.

When we arrived at Wells, the tide was a long way out and there were miles of flat, wet sand backed by dunes and fir trees, a wonderful place for children. We paddled and made sandcastles and then we all piled into a small boat and were rowed out to the sand banks where we dug for cockles. I remember looking back at the land and thinking what a long way away it seemed and wondering a little nervously if the man

Doris and a little helper from the village shelling cockles, watched by John, 1936.

Mill Street. The mill was the tallest in Norfolk. Its sails actually turned over the mill house behind it. The man with the bicycle is Billy Gilding, general dealer.

don't know where he got it all from, or how many animals were needed to provide it, but every child was given suet. Occasionally Grandma bought some which she grated up to make a boiled suet pudding, either filled with meat and kidney or apple and cinnamon.

Another regular caller was Mr Milford, the grocer, who had a car with a trailer on the back and came down the Drift once a week. Sometimes Grandma would go down to the gate to see what he had to offer and sometimes he would come up the path and sit in the kitchen while Grandma went over her shopping list with him. If he did not have what she wanted on the trailer, he would promise to see if he could bring it

the following week. It was not only food he sold; on one occasion he arrived with a telescope. My brother had asked for one for his birthday and Mr Milford had found one for him. Mr Haze Howlett, who kept the bakery beside the mill, delivered the bread by horse and cart. There is a story that one day one of his horses bolted into Bees Pit in Mill Street, so it seems such a thing was not an uncommon occurrence.

One year the rivers and ponds were teeming with fish and the pit in Black Drift was no exception. A huge pike lived there; everyone knew it was there and many an angler had tried to catch it with a variety of bait, but it defied them all. My grandfather watched its habits and knew where it liked

Walter with the pike taken from the pit, 1930s.

to hide and one day he went down to the pit from the orchard side and cast a line in. He sat there a long time and his patience was rewarded when he reeled the fish in and brought it home on the end of a pole slung over his shoulder.

There were two weddings in 1938, Gladys married William Dent and went to live at Wroxham, and Emma married Ray Barnes and they made their home at Great Dunham. The latter was a wedding I remember vividly because I was a bridesmaid and John a page boy. Our mother took us to Necton the day before the ceremony and we were met at the station, as usual, by Grandad with the pony and trap.

I slept very little that night and woke early. It was a beautiful sunny morning, but I was feeling very sick and in no condition to appreciate it. 'What she needs is a little fresh air and something to take her mind off it,' my grandmother said.

'Well, she can't go out to play, she'll get filthy,' my mother said.

'She can go with Pa. He's going to pick up the flowers.'

And so I was put in the pony and trap and my grandfather and I set off for Swaffham where Grandad pulled up outside the florist's shop and fetched a bouquet for the bride, posies for the bridesmaids and several pink carnation buttonholes, which he put on the seat beside me. But instead of turning the trap round and going straight home, he moved on and pulled up outside the pub.

'You bide there,' he said, looping the reins round a nearby post, 'An' don't jiffle[20] about or you'll set the hoss off. I'll not be long.' With that, he disappeared inside the pub. I don't suppose there was much risk of

the pony taking off, it knew where its master was and would not leave without him, but I was nervous enough to sit very still indeed. Grandad must have mentioned that I was waiting for him in the trap outside because after a little while he came out, lifted me down and took me inside. I was given a seat in the corner and a glass of lemonade and told to sit quietly and be a good girl.

A little while later, with Grandad fortified, we set off home. 'No call to let on where we're bin,' he said almost offhandedly. 'There's too much 'citement in the house a'ready. You jes' keep squat.'

As soon as we arrived, Grandad was packed off to the hut to change into a suit and a collar and tie and I was bundled upstairs to be helped into my pink dress and to have my hair brushed again. By that time Mr Hubbard was at the gate with his car and there was another one just behind him. It was such a rush I completely forgot about being sick.

Back at the smallholding after the ceremony, there was a feast and a big white cake and the usual photographs outside the door. I suspect my grandmother guessed where my grandfather had taken me; it was not easy to deceive her and his breath must have smelled of the ale he had drunk. No doubt, if she said anything to him, it was said in private.

My grandparents seemed somewhat preoccupied when we were there in the summer of 1939 and spent more time than usual listening to the wireless, a large cumbersome affair powered by accumulators. It had always lived on the cupboard in the alcove of the sitting room, but had been brought into the kitchen and stood on a

[20]fidget

small cane table to be more easily listened to. It crackled and whistled so much you had to give it your undivided attention if you wanted to hear anything; it was certainly no good for background music. But no one bothered about that; the wireless was purely functional, its chief purpose, as far as my grandparents were concerned, was the dissemination of news. I gathered that something unusual was happening in the outside world that, to my mind, in no way affected Necton.

The weather that summer was glorious and Philip had joined us for part of our holiday, which gave us even more opportunities for finding mischief. Leaving the adults to their listening, we went off down the Drift, coming back when we judged it was time to eat and that was usually our only reason for returning. Expecting a 'mobbing' from Aunt Norah for being late, we found her busy with a tape measure, sizing up the tiny windows.

'What are you doing?' I asked her.

'Measuring for blackout material.'

'What's that?'

'Never mind, dinner's ready. Sit down and get on with it.'

We needed no second invitation and began to tuck in to meat pie and vegetables with appetites sharpened by hours out of doors, listening to the conversation of the adults, which was peppered with words like 'blackout', 'rationing' and 'the last lot'. Remembering my grandmother's stories, my ears pricked up at this, but I was not unduly concerned. Necton was not a place to worry in. It was a kind of haven of peace, where you could spend hours doing absolutely nothing and yet the time flew by.

As soon as we children had finished, we dashed off again. We were dawdling down the Drift, past the pit with its ducks in the middle and its weeds and refuse on the edge, when Philip told us his mother was due on the afternoon train. Who first thought of the idea I cannot remember, but we decided we would all go and meet her at Holme Hale station, which is where Grandad always went with the pony and trap to meet visitors. I cannot remember whether we entirely discounted the fact that he might go as usual, or that we thought he would catch us up and we could all travel home together. It is more likely that we did not think about it at all.

Instead of turning for home as we should have done, we continued down the Drift and out on to the Holme Hale road. Here we crossed the road and scrambled through a hedge near the house that had once been the Jolly Farmers, the inn my great-grandparents had kept, but which had been delicensed in 1910 and had since become a private dwelling. From there we crossed a field and came out on to a narrow hedge-lined lane with a shallow ford running across it. I think there might have been a footbridge, but if there was, we did not use it and paddled through the water.

By the time we reached the station, which was only a tiny wayside halt with a stationmaster, ticket collector and porter all in one, Ann was beginning to tire, but we chivvied her along and said she would be able to rest while we waited for the train. But we had been walking quite a long while and the train had already been signalled. We stood on the platform in a line, eagerly peering into every carriage as it slowed and stopped in a hiss of steam. Aunt Rachel was sitting on the side of the carriage that looked out on to the platform and seeing four children jumping up and down, her own son among them, she hastily stood up, grabbed her case and scrambled out of the train just as it was pulling away again.

'What on earth are you doing here?' she greeted us. 'Is Grandad here with the trap?'

'No. We walked.'

'Walked!' She stared at us in disbelief. 'All of you? Even Ann?'

'Yes.'

'Good God!' This was followed by a severe scolding because Aunt Rachel had known my grandfather was unable to meet her and had arranged to go on to Swaffham and hire a car to take her to Necton from there. Seeing us on the platform, she had had no choice but to leave the train and now we were all going to have to walk home. By this time Ann was beginning to cry. The prospect of that long walk back was daunting and her feet were hurting her. Aunt Rachel sat her on the bank and took off her wet shoes and socks. The poor child had an enormous blister on her heel.

'Philip, you run home and tell them what's happened, get someone down here to help. I can't carry Ann all that way and it's obvious she can't walk.'

Philip set off at a trot, leaving me to bear the brunt of my aunt's anger. We rested a while, then continued a little way with Aunt Rachel carrying Ann and John and I struggling with her case between us, but we could not carry on like that and so we sat on the grass at the side of the road and waited. I was getting tired myself and hoped Grandad would arrive with the pony and trap, but it was Uncle Arthur who came with his bicycle. He strapped my aunt's case on the carrier at the back, sat Ann on the cross bar and cycled off, leaving my Aunt, my brother and I to continue on foot. As an adventure it had been a dreadful flop and I never heard the last of it.

It was one of my grandfather's rules that whatever mischief the children got up to it was the eldest who was at fault for leading the others astray. It was a rule all his children knew; it was intended to give the older ones a sense of responsibility, but I suffered from a terrible feeling of injustice because I was only six days older than Philip. And anyway, he was a boy.

We had all settled down again by the time Aunt Norah returned with a brown paper parcel, which she unwrapped on the kitchen table. It contained yards and yards of black cotton material. 'Would you credit it, I had to queue up for this,' she said. 'I thought I was going to miss the bus home.'

'No doubt there'll be queues for everything before much longer,' my grandmother said. 'I mind the last time, someone would say the butcher hev sausages and afore you could blink, there'd be a queue a mile long.'

'Perhaps we should get some stocks in,' my aunt suggested as she spread the material out and began cutting it into lengths. 'You never know...'

'Maybe, but surely they'll have learned from what happened last time and start rationing straight off.' She poked the fire in the kitchen range and then took the lid off the top with a special hook in order to settle the kettle over the flames.

My grandfather came in soon after that; the material was cleared away and the table laid for tea and not long after eating, we children were sent to bed. We lay awake for a long time talking about our day's adventures. We were not then at all concerned about the wider issues of war and all that would mean.

Two days later Aunt Rachel took Philip home and it was to be many years before I saw him again.

Before the end of the holiday Grandma disappeared for a whole day and night. While she was gone Aunt Norah fetched out the sewing machine, which was kept in the cupboard by the fireplace in the sitting room, and set about making blackout curtains for all the windows. When I asked her where Grandma was, I was told she had gone to see Aunt Emma. 'You're going to have a new little cousin.'

Grandma returned in the middle of the following morning. I heard my aunt ask how things had gone. 'It's a boy. Ronald,' she said. 'They're both well.'

After a cup of tea, she went to lie down for an hour or two but was soon busy again, helping with the blackout curtains. She remembered those early Zeppelin raids when the enemy had dropped their bombs wherever they saw a light on the ground and she was determined that not the tiniest glimmer of a candle flame would send its message up into the sky, if she could help it.

Two mornings later, when I came down for breakfast, she was missing again. To my enquiry my aunt said. 'She's gone to your Uncle Arthur's. You've got a new little cousin.'

'You mean another one?'

'Yes. A little girl this time.'

I kept watch for my grandmother's return and as soon as I saw her cycling down the Drift, ran to meet her. 'I know where you've been,' I called out, taking the bicycle and wheeling it up the path for her. 'Uncle Arthur's got a new baby girl and you had to be there when she came.'

'Now, how do you know that?'

'Aunt Norah told me.' For the news to have preceded her home, someone must have come down the Drift earlier, probably Mrs Powley or Dolly.

Later my uncle came and I ran to the garden gate to meet him. 'You've got a new baby girl and she's our cousin.'

'That's right,' he said. 'Do you want to come home alonga me to see her?'

'Oh, yes, please.'

He stopped to speak to my grandparents for a few minutes and then put me on his crossbar and we cycled up the village to Watery Lane, where he now lived. The army had taken over Necton Hall and as job and house went together, Arthur had to move and was now working at Bowman's model toy factory in East Dereham. The small row of houses had a brook running along the front of it and we had to cross a little bridge to get to his front door. Here I made the acquaintance of my cousin, Dulcie. A few days later Emma brought Ronald down to see us and by that time my mother had arrived to take us home.

We had no sooner arrived back in London than we learned that as many children as possible were being evacuated from the capital. Our father wanted to send us to our Canadian relatives, where we would be safe from bombing, but Mother put her foot down. Later, she was very glad she did when the news came that one of the ships taking children to America had been torpedoed. On the other hand she did not want us to be sent to some anonymous address in the country with the rest of the school and so my grandmother offered to have us. Within a week of leaving Necton we were on our way back. 'There's going to be a war,' Mother told us. 'You'll be going to school in Necton.'

This was startling news and greeted with mixed feelings. How would we get on if we had to live here all the time? Would we be treated any differently? And what would it be like going to Necton school with all the other village children? And what about our parents? What would they be doing? If we had not always been so content at Necton, I doubt if we would have accepted the situation with quite the same measure of equanimity.

Grandad met us as usual, giving no indication either by word or deed, what he thought of this new turn of events. Having the children for a few days' holiday was hardly the same as having them for months on end; he no more believed the optimists who said it would be over by Christmas than he had those who had said it at the beginning of the Great War.

We took the dog for a run down the Drift and fed the hens and the pony, but in the back of our minds was the thought that this was no holiday and that Necton was to become our home. It did not stop me sleeping that night, but I was thinking of it the next morning when I went downstairs.

Before I could sit down for breakfast, we heard Mr Larwood's pony and trap stop at the gate. Grandma took a large enamel jug down from the shelf and handed it to me. 'Go and fetch the milk for me, there's a good girl.'

I took the jug down to the gate because Mr Larwood did not come up to the door

and he certainly did not deliver the milk in bottles. He had two large farm churns on the back of the trap and a couple of tin measures with handles that hooked on the side of the churn, one held a pint and the other a quart. He dipped the quart measure into one of the churns and tipped the frothing contents into the jug I held. 'Yer still here, then?' he commented. 'Not gone back to owd London?'

'No, I'm going to stay and go to school in Necton.'

'Oh, yer'll larn a tidy bit there, I don't doubt.'

I did not know how to answer him and just said, 'Thank you', as I carefully carried the milk back into the kitchen.

That night we were woken by a particularly noisy thunderstorm; rain was beating on the window pane and bright flashes of lightning lit the sky. The dog began to bark and Ann put her head under the bedcovers. John and I scrambled out of bed to look.

Grandma must have heard the floorboards creaking because she came up the stairs and sent us scurrying back to bed, before she threw a towel over the mirror and told us to go back to sleep. Although she told us there was nothing to be afraid of, it was God's way of bringing the rain, she always covered the mirrors and hid the knives in a drawer when there was lightning about. We woke next morning to bright sunshine with hardly a cloud in the sky.

My mother returned to London the following day and by then the Prime Minister, Neville Chamberlain, had made his historic broadcast and everyone realised that the war to end all wars had been nothing of the sort and the country was going to have to go through it all again.

World War II

IT WAS GLOOMY in the little cottage because for once the door was shut. Outside it was freezing. Even so, my grandfather was out. He always found plenty to do, looking after his animals, and was rarely indoors, though he had begun taking a little nap on the sofa after lunch – his only concession to getting older.

I was endeavouring to finish the dish-cloth I was knitting for my mother and my brother was sitting at the table making paper chains out of strips of paper cut from magazine covers and any paper that had colourful pictures. He was being helped by Ann, whose little fingers seemed to be covered in the flour paste Grandma had made. Grandma was plucking a large cockerel, sitting on a low chair close to the hearth with it held firmly between her knees while she pulled out the feathers by the handful.

Everyone had helped make the Christmas pudding weeks before, stirring it with a wooden spoon and making a wish. 'I don't know what it'll be like,' she had said, pouring a glass of sherry – 'brown milk' she always called it – into the mixture. 'It's got more carrots and apples than dried fruit in it.' But in spite of what she said, it did have quite a lot of fruit, because both she and my mother had been hoarding it for just this purpose and my mother had sent her share down by post. It also contained a good dash of alcohol and several silver threepenny bits. The pudding had been boiled for hours in the copper and was now standing in the wash house wearing a new pudding cloth tied on with string. It would have its final boiling on Christmas morning.

We had just finished our first term at Necton school, which was very different from our London school. According to Aunt Norah it was exactly the same as it had been when she went there: the same big classrooms, the same pot-bellied stove, the guard of which was still used to dry off the children's wet clothes and which periodically collapsed with a clatter. There were the same unsavoury toilets out in the playground, with 'girls' engraved over one door and 'boys' over the other and the same strict discipline.

Mrs Clarke had retired and Mr Birtwistle was now headmaster. He taught the older pupils in a separate room, while the rest were taught by two lady teachers who shared the big room. Because of the shortage of paper, some of the old slates of our mother's day had been unearthed for us to use, which was fine because it was easy to rub out our mistakes. Those exercise books we did have were treated with reverence. We had to take brown paper or old wallpaper to school to cover them and every page had to be numbered as soon as the book was issued, which put an end to the practice of secretly tearing out pages that contained too many errors and starting again.

It was not only the shortages that made life difficult for Mr Birtwistle. The village was hosting about 50 London evacuees and the school was being shared with them and the two teachers who had come with them. The village children, and that included my brother and me who were not official evacuees, went to school from eight in the morning to half past twelve and the Londoners went in the afternoons, which suited us down to the ground. It meant we could have the afternoons to ourselves.

The evacuees were billeted all over the village, but because we were staying with my grandmother, she was not required to have them. Vi Fickling had seven, all boys, many of whom kept in touch with her after the war. Some of the children, in the country for the first time, had never seen a cow and ran from them in fright, others were afraid to paddle in case the minnows swam over their feet. Some fell in the dykes and Grandad kept a close eye on any children he saw going anywhere near the pit. He was gruff with them and his dialect was so strange I think he terrified them. On the other hand he could be very kind and often had an apple from the orchard in his pocket to give them.

Every day, along with our gas masks, we each took a teaspoon to school with us to be dosed with cod liver oil and malt. We had a third of a pint of milk every day during our playtime break too, for which we payed 2½d a week.

We were sent to Sunday School though we did not want to go any more than my mother had done, especially when the common was so near and inviting. We would wander over its springy turf for hours, looking for birds' nests, picking flowers, gathering nuts and crab apples, falling into cow pats and scratching our hands and faces on brambles. On the day my brother cut his foot rather badly on a piece of glass when we were paddling in the brook, we knew the game was up. According to my grandfather, it was all my fault. I was the eldest.

I had another battle with him because I am what he contemptuously called cack-handed, and he was determined I should put my pudding spoon in my right hand to eat and I was equally determined I would not. I sat looking at a congealing plate of apple dumpling and custard the whole afternoon. When the time came to lay the table for tea, it was whisked away by Grandma before Grandad came back and nothing more was said. But I am left wondering who had actually won. I had not used my right hand, but on the other hand I had been forced to sit still all afternoon when I might have been out enjoying myself.

On another occasion Grandad insisted on John eating his sprouts, telling him he would sit there until he had eaten at least one. John stuffed a cold sprout in his mouth, whereupon he was allowed to get down and go out to play. When we sat down to tea, Grandma noticed his bulging cheek and asked him, 'What have you got in your mouth?' He did not reply, so she made him open his mouth and hooked out a sprout, which he had held there the whole afternoon. It would have been long forgotten if he had swallowed it, but that meant my grandfather would have won the battle of wills and John was determined he would not.

If he really wanted to punish a recalcitrant child Grandad had more subtle ways. One day John played truant from school and spent the morning wandering round the fields. Knowledge of his crime preceded him home – someone had told Grandad they had seen him. This time there was no unbuckling of his belt, no shouting. He simply fetched the little Windsor chair and set it down outside the front door, where he commanded John to sit in it and think about what he had done. He was not allowed to have anything in his hands, no small toy, no book, not even the contents of his pockets, which were confiscated. He had to sit there with nothing to do and nothing to look at but the fields and the sky, until bedtime. It was a punishment he has never forgotten, so one can assume it was effective.

We were not unhappy at all, but we did miss our parents and it was not like being on holiday. But they were coming to join us for Christmas and as the holiday approached we grew more and more excited.

On Christmas Eve, while I helped Grandma to make mince pies, being given the paper from the lard packet to grease the tins ready for the pastry, Grandad went to meet them with the pony and trap. It was warm as toast in the house, but outside there were already a few flakes of snow drifting down, and we were speculating on the chances of a white Christmas. Aunt Norah came in with an armful of holly and ivy and a couple of sprigs of mistletoe cut from one of the apple trees, which she used to decorate the two downstairs rooms. It was considered very bad luck to bring the greenery into the house before Christmas Eve, just as it was unlucky to burn it afterwards. On twelfth night, it would be taken down, one piece would be put in the back

of the kitchen cupboard to keep good luck in the house and a sprig of mistletoe would be hung in the cowshed to bring fertility to the cows; the rest was thrown into the hedge in the orchard to rot down naturally.

The mince pies were coming hot from the oven just as our parents arrived. 'Come you on in, t'gether,' my grandmother greeted them, while we ran to be hugged and kissed. 'It's fare freezin' out there.'

We were allowed a mince pie for our tea and after that we decorated the tree with ginger bread men, sugar mice and tiny coloured candles. Then it was time to go to bed and hang up our socks – no pillow cases for us. We woke long before it was light and crept to the end of the bed to feel what had been put in them. We dare not light a candle and had to wait until dawn when we could open the blackout curtains to see what the socks contained. We each had an apple, a bag of sweets, a few nuts, a chocolate Father Christmas, a colouring book and some crayons.

I have often wondered where we all slept. I think my parents must have had our grandparents' bed in the hut because when I wandered downstairs, far too early for the adults in the house, my grandmother was curled up on the horsehair sofa, covered with an eiderdown. Of my grandfather there was no sign. Did he sleep in the stable? Or had he spent the night somewhere else in the village? He was certainly there at breakfast time.

It was a wonderful Christmas; the war seemed a million miles away. We had presents from all the adults, jigsaws, handkerchiefs, gloves, slippers. From my parents I had a stamp album with a few stamps, John had a model aeroplane kit and Ann a doll's teaset. My rather unevenly knitted dishcloth was received by my mother with every appearance of pleasure. Other members of the family arrived during the day and were offered a glass of sherry or beer. The leaves were pulled out of the dining room table in the best room for it to be laid up for dinner and the chicken and its stuffing, with roast potatoes, sprouts and gravy, disappeared amidst great jollity. This was the first Christmas of the war, though the expected air raids had not materialised and, except for some shortages, we did not seem to be particularly affected. Many of the evacuees were drifting back home and my parents spoke of having us home too, but then decided to leave us a little longer to see what happened.

They went back to London the day after Boxing Day and we were left behind to see in the New Year at Necton, which was heralded in the time-honoured way with Uncle Arthur acting as 'first foot'. No one was allowed to leave the house between midnight and his arrival very early on the morning of 1 January, bearing a lump of coal, a piece of bread and a small bag of salt, all intended to bring good luck and prosperity in the coming year. Grandma always maintained she did not believe such nonsense, but she would no more have discontinued the old practices than fly. I suppose it was the old belt and braces approach. You did your best to do what was right and look after those around you, but you needed a little bit of luck as well and you did not do anything to tempt providence.

The winter really set in after New Year. It was the coldest January since Eliza and Alice had played with a toboggan at the brickworks, almost half a century before.

Wrapped up warm in woolly coats, pixie hoods and knitted mittens, we went down the Drift to the pit and stood laughing as the ducks slid helplessly across it. Some of the village children ventured on it to make slides; some even found old skates and wobbled about on it until Grandad came dashing down the Drift and yelled at them to come off. Poor Grandad felt the weight of his responsibilities over that small stretch of water.

We woke up one morning to a blanket of snow and what was worse, it had drifted and those of us who lived down Black Drift were cut off, as were other small hamlets and isolated farms. Grandad and Norah cleared the path to the gate and the end shed, where Grandad found some old snow shoes. Aunt Norah tied them to her boots and set off across the meadow to the village to buy what essentials we needed, paraffin for the lamps and recharged accumulators to power the wireless, our only contact with the outside world.

We children had a wonderful time building snowmen, throwing snowballs and floundering in the drifts, which were deep enough to swallow us. It was not quite so much fun visiting the privy or getting out of bed in the mornings when the inside of the window was as frozen as the outside and the water on the washstand had a thin film of ice on it, but we had to put up with that and, for the most part, dressed under the bedclothes.

'As the days lengthen, so the cold strengthen,' my grandmother quoted when we complained. 'It's fare better than a green churchyard.'

'What does that mean?'

'A green churchyard is a full churchyard,'

she said. 'A mild winter don't kill off the bugs and there always seems to be more illness about.'

I loved hearing my grandmother's sayings and tales of days gone by. She was always equating those times with the present, especially the war, comparing prices and the way things were done. It was strange how many similarities there were. There was a strict blackout and fears about bombing, though now, of course, it was not Zeppelins we were expecting but aeroplanes. There were queues and rumours of spies and posters proclaiming 'careless talk costs lives'.

The farmers were once again being exhorted to plough up grassland to grow more food and, once again, some were losing their land for so-called incompetence. Many farm workers, fed up with low wages, were leaving to join up or work in the factories or to help build new aerodromes, just as they had a quarter of a century before. And just as before, the exodus left the farms short of workers. Again there were Pig Clubs and wartime recipes, one of which was Wootton Pie, a kind of shepherd's pie without the meat, which was named after the Minister of Food of the time. We heard the recipes on the wireless, in programmes like the *Kitchen Front* with Freddie Grisewood and Mabel Constanduros. And again the children were organised into collecting medicinal herbs from the hedgerows: nettles, foxgloves, rose hips, acorns, horse chestnuts and raspberry leaves. The rose hips were made into syrup for nursing mothers and babies and tannic acid was extracted from conkers to make cream and lotions for the treatment of burns. Although we were paid a few coppers, I do not remember making much money from this, so I expect the novelty soon wore off.

My grandmother's hope that the government would learn the lessons of the last war, were to some extent realised when some rationing was introduced that January. We had already been registered and issued with National Identity and ration cards when sugar, butter, bacon and ham were all rationed. Grandad had a pig and a few cows, so the only thing we really had to watch was the sugar. No one was allowed sugar in their tea.

Grandma was registered with Mr Milford for groceries, who still called with his car and trailer and marked up our ration books. The baker still brought the bread, sometimes coming on a bicycle with a big carrier on the front containing his basket. He would prop the bike against the wall, lift out the basket and bring it up to the house for Grandma to make her choice, which before long consisted of nothing but the National Loaf (to save wheat flour it was mixed with flour from barley and oats and this turned it grey; white bread became a thing of the past) and occasionally a Hovis. Bread was not rationed, but the lovely white crusty loaves we had enjoyed before and the iced buns we had for a special treat soon disappeared.

Another regular caller was the postwoman, who was none other than my grandmother's great friend Vi Fickling. It was a job she had done for years and would do for many more. Vi was out in all weathers, cycling round the village with the mail and passing the time of day with everyone. There was hardly a day went by when she did not come down Black Drift with post and then she would stop for a cup of tea before going on again. She brought mail from Alfred, Gladys and Audrey, from Great Aunt Sarah and from my mother and Alice, whose letters were once again having to run the gauntlet of enemy shipping. John, the elder of her two sons, had joined the Royal Canadian Regiment almost as soon as war was declared and was in Europe somewhere, but she had no idea where.

While we were staying at Necton, we were always encouraged to write to our parents. After lunch on a Sunday, Grandma would go to the old bread oven, which served as a stationery cupboard, and extract a lined notepad, a bottle of ink, a steel-nibbed pen for me and a pencil for John, and sit us down at the table in the front room. We would rather have been doing other things, chasing each other down the Drift or taking the dog for a walk, but those pursuits on a Sunday were frowned upon. 'Besides,' she told us 'your Mum and Dad like to hear what you've bin a-doin'.' We knew we would not get our freedom until we complied, so we dutifully racked our brains for something to say. Invariably we ended, 'Grandad and Grandma and Aunt Norah send their love. Hope you are well. Love...'

Grandma would read it through and perhaps add a sentence or two of her own and the paper, pen and ink would be returned to the oven. The envelope would be written and stamped and then we were sent to the top of the Drift to put it in the post box.

One balmy spring day when daffodils were nodding their heads in the patch of flower garden beside the hut and the gillyflowers were filling the air with their scent, Molly Clements appeared at the open back door, just as we were sitting down to our midday meal. The Clements family lived across the Drift and Molly was about my age. 'Please, Mrs Ong,' she said. 'Mum says can you let her have a sheet of notepaper, she do want to write a letter.'

Grandma left the table and fetched the notepad from the cupboard and handed it to Molly. 'Tell Mum to take what she needs.'

We had just started on our pudding when Molly reappeared to return the pad. 'Mum says thank you very much and could you let her have an envelope?'

Grandma left the table, put the notepad away and fetched out an envelope, which she gave to Molly, who disappeared at a trot. She was back just as we were finishing our meal.

'Mum says thank you and could you oblige her with a stamp?'

This was the last straw for my grandfather. He looked up at Molly, who was already half afraid of him, and said, 'Ask yar Ma if she'd like me to lick it and stick it on for her. An' then mayhap, she'd like me to tek it up the rud and put it in the box.' Molly fled and we never knew if this message was passed on or, if it was, how it was received.

I would sometimes be sent to the shop in Ivy Todd with a shopping list, a purse containing some money, our ration books and a string bag to bring home my purchases. The shop was kept by two spinster ladies called Green and was no more than the front room of their little house. It was gloomy inside because the tiny window was so full of posters, packets, jars and tins,

The brick building in the middle is the little shop in Ivy Todd that was kept by Winnie and Dorothy Green. It is now a private house.

they blocked what little light there was. The room was lined with shelves and crammed with everything the ladies thought their customers might need: tins of fruit and sardines, now fast disappearing off the shelves; sugar in sacks, which was dispensed into blue paper bags for anyone who was registered there; boot polish and laces, candles, matches and paraffin; sewing thread, buttons and pins; ink and writing paper; string and lamp wicks. And jars and jars of sweets: boiled sweets, humbugs, peppermints, liquorice sticks and sherbet dabs, as well as cardboard boxes opened up to display small bars of chocolate, none of which were rationed at that point in the war.

I was always allowed to spend a halfpenny on myself 'for going' and making a choice from all these goodies occupied some time. 'Come on, Mary, make up your mind,' the elder Miss Green would say, as I dithered. When I had made my choice and handed over the money, my purchases were packed into the string bag for me to take home. But before I went I was taken behind the counter to the back room to see the colourful parrot the Misses Green kept there. On good days we could persuade it to say 'Pretty Polly.'

Later in the war, after I had gone home, my sister did the shopping and always, when she handed it over to my grandmother, she would say, 'I spent a penny on myself for going.' There's inflation for you.

Easter arrived and with it hot cross buns and Easter eggs, which were not the chocolate variety but real eggs laid by the hens in the orchard.

'One time eggs were forbidden in Lent,' Grandma told us, 'an' that was why evraone hev pancakes on Shrove Tuesday to use the eggs up afore Lent. It finish on Easter Sunday and that was when you could have eggs again an' because it were such a treat, they were tricolated.'[21]

She showed us what she meant by boiling some eggs in onion skins until they were hard, which gave them a mottled lemon colour. Some of the eggs she wrapped in cheap red ribbon saved from the Christmas parcels before boiling them and the dye from the ribbon coloured the shells. After that she made up several different coloured dyes: red came from cochineal, green from spinach and yellow from saffron. 'If there isn't any saffron, gorse blossom is just as good,' she said.

'And it's always in bloom,' I put in, remembering her earlier tales.

A newspaper was spread on the front room table and we spent hours decorating those eggs, knowing Mother was coming to stay for a few days and would be with us that afternoon. While we painted away, Grandma cooked. I think she was convinced that my mother, not having the bounty of the countryside, was probably starving and needed fattening up. Mother only stayed a few days, not wanting to leave my father too long.

The war was not going well. The Germans were striding across Europe and it did not seem as if anyone could stop them. Denmark and Norway were followed by Holland and Belgium. Chamberlain resigned and Winston Churchill became Prime Minister and made his famous 'blood, toil, tears and sweat' speech and everyone rallied behind him. A new optimism swept the country. There had been no air raids and the trickle of evacuees returning to London became a flood. At Whitsun my mother came and fetched me home.

The optimism that had sparked off my return to London, along with many other evacuees was premature. Dunkirk was a magnificent disaster and in June the Germans marched into Paris in triumph and then began bombing the airfields of southern England, but it was not long before they turned their attention to London and the blitz began. At the end of term, Mother took me back to Necton and left me there.

Nothing in Necton seemed to have changed. John and Ann were rosy-cheeked and obviously thriving. We did as we always had done, wandered round the village and down the Drift, getting into mischief.

Tea was rationed now and so was meat, at 1s 10d worth a week for an adult and half that for a child, but there were plenty of eggs, though the egg ration was forfeit for the privilege of keeping a limited number of chickens. There were plenty of home-grown vegetables and fruit, of course. 'An apple a day keep the doctor away,' my grandmother said. Oranges, lemons and bananas disappeared for the duration of the war. Some children grew up never having tasted them. The pig disappeared that holiday and a few days later we enjoyed roast pork for Sunday lunch and

---

[21]decorated

bacon for our breakfast. Later in the week there were sausages.

'Before the war,' Grandma said. 'If you had a pig, it hatta to go to the butcher to be slaughtered and sold, but now, if we've had it two months, we kin hev the carcass for ourselves.' Without refrigeration the meat could not be kept for any length of time. What was not immediately used was distributed to friends and neighbouring farmers who reciprocated when they killed their own animals, which they tried to do at different times. I remember everyone had a swill bucket that was emptied into a cart at regular intervals by someone from the nearest pig farm. There was one outside the door of the school where we could put the cores of the apples we had brought to school to eat with our milk.

We did not go to the seaside that year. For one thing Mr Hubbard could not get the petrol for such jaunts and for another, the beaches had been mined against invasion. But to give my grandmother a rest and give us a change of scenery, and perhaps because she did not want to deprive our Yorkshire cousins of their summer holiday at Necton, we spent some of the time with other relatives. It may also have been that Grandma had been booked for a birth. Now and again, she would say it was time she stopped, but could not bring herself to refuse when she was asked to attend.

Another midwives' act had been passed in 1936, which provided for a salaried midwifery service subsidised by the government, but it was still not free. The fee had to be collected from the patients by the midwife and passed on to the Local Supervisory Authority, but there were still many women who could not pay or begrudged the money and did not book the official midwife, preferring to call in my grandmother. Those who gave birth when the midwife was off-duty or on holiday, naturally turned to her. By now she was over 60, her family had grown up and the need to earn a few coppers was not so urgent, but there was more than enough work for two and the local doctors still liked to have her around. She may not have been quite so busy, but she was certainly not redundant.

At the end of the holiday, John went back to school in Necton and I was taken to Swaffham station in the pony and trap. I was put on a train in the care of the guard, who was instructed to see that I changed at Ely and got on the connection to Liverpool Street where my mother would meet me. With petrol like gold dust, the trains were packed, but the guard found me a seat. I was a little apprehensive that my mother would be prevented from meeting me, but she was standing anxiously at the barrier when the train drew in.

I discovered I was not to stay in London as it was still being bombed, and a few days later, I was put on the train to go to my Aunt Audrey at Eccles Road. I spent the next 15 months with my aunt, going to school in the village and making a whole host of new friends.

In spite of Churchill's rousing speeches, which everyone listened to along with such programmes as the *Kitchen Front*, *Itma*, *Mind My Bike* and *Sandy's Half Hour* of organ music, 1941 was the most depressing of the war. Overseas, the army was fighting in the desert and at home the air raids continued. London was not the only place to be bombed – almost every major town was hit. Norwich had been hit early in July and there were some casualties and considerable damage. On the last day of August, a heavy force of bombers had come over the eastern counties, targeting airfields and frightening everyone to death. Six soldiers were killed at Swaffham station in a daylight bombing raid and we were thankful that no one from the family was travelling at that time. But the end of the war was a long way off and we were to do a great deal more travelling before we were all reunited again.

Looking After the Grandchildren

ELIZA LOVED all her grandchildren and enjoyed having them to stay, but looking after two of them for months on end must have been a heavy responsibility, especially as my brother, in the way of all small boys, was always getting into scrapes. Skinned knees, glass in his foot, tumbling into stinging nettles, cuts, bruises and bumps on the head were commonplace and dealt with by our grandmother as part and parcel of her duty of care.

On one occasion John and Ann were playing with Molly Clements and wandered into her father's shed, where sacks of grain and seed were stored. I cannot believe they were truly hungry, but all three took handfuls

Doris with Walter, Ann and John.

of the seed beans and ran into the Drift to hide themselves behind the end shed, where they tucked in. The result was that they were all very ill that night. 'We didn't need our usual dose of syrup of figs,' my brother told me later.

The sound of them getting out of bed and their groans brought Grandma up the stairs to see what was wrong. Her first question was 'What have you been eating?' But guilt or fear made them keep silent. She suggested things like deadly nightshade and laburnum or perhaps they had eaten some toadstools in mistake for mushrooms, but they denied everything. The cramps continued all night and Grandma sat with them, thinking that she would have to call in the doctor and worrying about what she would tell my mother. But at last the pain eased and they drifted off to sleep.

Next day my grandmother learned from Mrs Clements that Molly had also been very ill, though neither woman could think what had caused it. It was not until she was crossing the Drift to return home that Grandma saw the pile of bean shells behind the end shed. It relieved her mind to know it was nothing she had given the children to eat and as they seemed to have taken no harm, she did no more than give them a scolding.

On another occasion she took John to the doctor when he had fallen and a large splinter of wood had gone into his leg and defied her attempts to draw it out. I have a letter she wrote to my mother in April 1941, which provides a graphic picture of how things were:

My Dear Doris and Adrian
So sorry I have not got you a line off before to say we got your parcel safe on Sat morn.

How did you manage to get so much cake? Anyway the children liked them very much. Ann keep going to the tin to see how much is left. The sausages were nice, we had them for dinner, as I took them into Swaffham as you will see by John's letter. I took him to Dr Moss and he got the splinter out and John want to send it for you to see. It wasn't a big job, he soon found it and said had it been a piece of green wood he would have had more trouble with it. It's all right now.

I got him a nice pair of shoes, black again, as I did not like the brown ones, and a nice pair of sandals for Ann. Something new in a shade of light fawn, rather nice, they will come in later on. Now, my dear, I shall be glad when I get a line from you to know if you are all right and how you got on last week. By what I hear you have had a busy time of it up there again. Hope it was not very near you. I did feel I wanted to wire you but then I thought it wouldn't do any good, so I put it no news is good news. I have been asked if you were all right as some of them sent news this way that they have lost everything, some of the Ashman's family. We had planes over all night long so thought there was something going on somewhere. Now you would like to know I got over my village job all right but what a lot of questions. I was asked if I saw anything unusual in the room. Anyway it ended up by heart failure and I was glad they took him to West Ham to be buried, so that's finished with. Well, dear, I don't think there is anything else for now so will end with lots of love and thank you for my little parcel. Your Mum and Dad.

The letter is stained brown where the wood splinter was pressed into the paper. My grandmother's reference to her village job I think refers to the fact she was called

> Black buff-
> Necton
>
> My dear Doris & Adrain   21/4/41
>   So sorry I have not got
> you a line off before to say we
> got your parcel safe on Sat morn
> how did you manage to get so much
> cake anyway the children liked
> them very much Ann keep going
> to the tin to see how much is
> left; the Sausages were nice we
> had them for dinner as I took
> them into Swaffham as you will
> see by Johns letter, I took him
> to the Nurse he got the splinter out
> as you will see as John want to
> send it for you to see it wasn't
> a big job he soon found it and
> said had it been a piece of
> green wood he would have had
> more trouble with it;

The letter from Eliza to Doris. The brown marks made by the splinter can still be seen in the bottom right hand corner.

out to a sudden death and there had to be an inquest, which she was required to attend. She had obviously been a little concerned about it.

The weather had been bad in the early part of the year and ploughing and sowing had been delayed. 'That comes with using them grut heavy tractors,' my grandfather said. 'Hosses would ha' got that turned over long afore now.' The wet weather was succeeded by a dry, cold spring followed by a drought. The new potato crop was late and suffered from blight. Jam, marmalade and golden syrup were rationed, so was cheese. Almost everything else went on 'points', a system

Mary, John and Ann on the garden path, 1939. Ann is sitting on the little chair that was used by all the children. The cat unwittingly provided meat for the table during hard times.

away,' Grandma shouted. John ran and shut the door and then ensued a chase of comic proportions as the cat ran under the table, round the furniture and scrambled over chairs, pursued by Grandma and my brother. Puss was hampered by her efforts to keep a tight hold of her catch, which was almost as big as she was. She had to drop it in the end and Grandma pounced. Next day there was rabbit stew for dinner. It was hard on the poor cat, who had only brought her catch back to be praised for her cleverness. She had always been left to enjoy her spoils before, but now she only got the scraps left on the plates.

of rationing that allowed the housewife to choose what she bought among those foods not already rationed. The meat ration was reduced.

My grandmother's answer to that was to take pigeons off the cat when she brought them back to the house and put them into the pot. On one occasion, the cat brought a rabbit back, dragging it up the path between her legs and into the house. Grandma tried to take it off her, but she eluded the outstretched hand and made for the door. 'Shut that door. Don't let her get

This was not the only ploy my grandmother used to keep the children fed. Ann remembers Grandad standing a pail of milk in the back place, which he had taken from the cow and was going to feed to the calf, though why the calf could not take it directly from the cow I do not know. It must have been a daily occurrence because Grandma had a large jug standing ready on the table and as soon as Grandad's back was turned, she filled it with milk and added water to the pail. It was done so swiftly it was obvious she had done it many times before. Seeing Ann watching her, she put her finger to her lips. 'Shush, not a word.' It was a hot summer resulting in a lot of milk going sour and my grandmother boiled what we left every night and stood it on the floor of the larder in jugs covered with a circle of muslin edged with blue beads. Sometimes, if milk went sour, she would make cottage cheese, hanging it in a muslin bag over a bowl in the back place until all the liquid had drained out of it, then she would season it and flavour it with herbs and everyone would have it with water cress for tea.

Shipping losses at this time were enormous; Malta was under siege, we were fighting in the desert, Yugoslavia had been occupied and the Germans had invaded Greece and Crete. A British offensive in the desert failed and the year ended with German troops outside the gates of Moscow, where only the Russian winter saved the inhabitants. Singapore fell in February 1942 and thousands of British troops were taken prisoner, many of them from the Norfolk Regiment and among them Great Aunt Sarah's son, Arthur. Soap was rationed together with sweets and chocolate and there was no tea ration for children under five. The basic petrol ration was abolished and petrol only became available to people who could prove they needed it for war work. The pony and trap became even more important.

Clothing was on a coupon system. We were allowed 66 coupons a year. It took 12 to buy a coat, 11 for a dress and a proportionate number for shoes, stockings and underclothes. Coupons were even needed for handkerchiefs. Everyone was exhorted to 'make do and mend', which made my grandmother smile. 'I ha' bin doing that all my life,' she said. News that someone had parachute silk would fly around and everyone would want a piece. An extraordinary number of nightdresses and underslips could be made from the silk of one parachute.

Norah in Women's Land Army dungarees.

Conscription had been extended to all men between the ages of 18 and 51. Emma's husband, Ray, was called up and so was Audrey's husband, Dick, who went

Norah, this time in Women's Land Army uniform.

into the Royal Artillery. In December all women between 19 and 51, except those looking after children, were required to register for national service and the next time I saw my Aunt Norah she was wearing the khaki breeches, green jumper and felt hat of the Women's Land Army.

By this time air raids were no longer nightly affairs and indeed, seemed to have stopped altogether, but in April and May, several historic cities like Canterbury, Bath, York and Norwich were bombed. Norwich railway station received a direct hit. Railway carriages, goods wagons, stores and workshops were engulfed. The bombers dropped incendiaries into the flames and made matters worse. Water, gas and electricity mains were severed. Food stores, pubs, factories, a laundry and a hospital were all destroyed. There were several casualties and over a thousand people made homeless. It was too close for comfort and worried my grandparents, who were beginning to wonder if anywhere was safe.

Mrs Milstead's niece, Brenda, travelled from Rollesby where she lived, to Necton the next day. 'The buses all had gas bags towed behind to eke out the petrol and they were very slow and smelly,' she told me. 'We left Rollesby at quarter to ten and got to Norwich at quarter to one. St Stephen's Street was rubble, with open drains smelling dreadful. Firemen were still lifting the dead and injured out of the houses. We caught a bus to Necton at two o'clock, arriving at the Three Tuns at a quarter past four, then walked into the village to my aunt's house.' A journey of some 50 miles had taken all day.

Hearing that York had been hit, Grandma was anxious about Alfred and his family. He was working in a sugar beet factory at the time. Only a few months before she had learned that he had been injured when a kiln had exploded at the factory. 'It's like history repeating itself,' she said, remembering what had happened to Charles half a century before. Alfred was in hospital for some time, but was home now and had returned to work. The news of the bombing sent her to the cupboard to fetch out her letter writing materials.

Eliza was relieved to hear that, because of the bombing, my father's factory was taking over the Marmet pram factory in Letchworth, Hertfordshire, and my parents were moving out of London. There was talk of my brother and sister going home. Eliza wrote:

My Dear Doris and Adrian

Many thanks for your letter of today. I guessed you had been doing too much. You must try and rest a bit now. Tell Adrian not to bother about coming for John this week, let him have another week, it will give you a chance of another week's rest or a little longer if it will help you, then perhaps you could come for him so as to look over his clothes to see what's worth taking back. It's not worth taking what is of no use to them but you will see how you get on. I should not be able to come at Whitsun with Ann, it would have to be before or after. They have asked about her going to school but I said she would go after the Whitsun holidays, so will leave it to you to do what you think best. You should not have bothered about sending me any money this week as I know you have had a lot to do with the moving. Now it's as bad as the other place for getting anything.

We seem to be in a funny old muddle just now, it seem the same everywhere. We had a very bad night here Sunday night all night long it did not cease. I was up, the children were awake too, but Dad kept in bed as he had such a cold and was sweating so much he was afraid too. I was glad when it was morning. It was better last night, got a good night's sleep and was glad too, as I have a nasty cold. It seem to settle in my back and have felt so sick with it but it's getting better now I am glad to say. There have been such a lot of people with colds, Dad's cold is not much better, he seem ill with his. He seem to have so many changes. One day it seem nearly gone then it come back as bad and it's such a job to get anything for it

now. I think the weather have a lot to do with it, don't you? Well, dear, I must finish or I lose the post and I want you to get this. Now try and get a little more rest and not bother for John this week, he is all right.
Love Mum and Dad.

Reading between the lines it is obvious she was worried about my grandfather, but at the same time concerned that my mother had not been well and anxious to reassure her. She was also feeling the strain herself, though I am quite sure she never complained of it. My parents decided that Ann and John would join me at Eccles Road, where Ann started school.

We were there together for only one term. At the end of it, our father arrived with Mr Milford in his car, for which he was charged 2s 6d, and took John and Ann back to Necton. My grandmother had been told she had to take some evacuees, unless she could give a good reason for not doing so and she had told the officials she could not oblige because she was expecting her grandchildren. 'The devil you know,' she said with a smile.

I enjoyed living with my aunt. Her bungalow was right on the edge of Snetterton airfield, which was taken over by the American Air Force. One day one of the airmen told my aunt they had some oranges that had gone past their best and they were wondering if wine could be made with them. My aunt laughed and said, yes, but you would need sugar. The result was that an American jeep arrived at the door with a sack of oranges and another of sugar, along with a quantity of bottles and corks. I do not think my aunt had realised she was expected to make the wine and there was so much fruit she did not know what to make it in. In the end it was put in the copper in the corner of the kitchen, where it fermented happily for weeks, causing a powerful aroma, before it was bottled. It turned out to be very good and the Americans loved it, allowing my aunt to keep a few bottles for herself.

When we went to Necton for Christmas, we took two bottles of the wine with us. The train, as usual was packed, but we managed to find seats and put our bags and cases on the rack over our heads. Aunt Audrey, with Angela on her knee, was soon in conversation with others in the carriage who were grumbling good-naturedly about shortages and air raids, when there was a loud explosion. Everyone screamed and ducked, convinced that we were being

bombed. It was only when we saw the dreadful orange mess dripping down from the luggage rack on to our heads that my aunt realised the jolting of the train had shaken up the wine and it had blown its cork. Some of the passengers, whose nerves had perhaps been frayed by bombing, were really upset, but others rocked with laughter, possibly more high-pitched that it would normally have been because of the relief they felt. We arrived at Necton covered in a sticky orange mess that took ages to clean up.

There were Americans in Necton too and my mother and Audrey were taken to a dance in Dunham by two airmen stationed at North Pickenham, who had 'borrowed' a jeep for the purpose. In my mother's words, they had a 'high old time' and after-

Chapel Lane from the top of Black Drift, 1952. Rest Cottage is on the right and the Powley's house is on the left.

wards they were given two huge joints of meat. My grandfather was furious. 'Married women, the pair on yer, actin' like Jezebels,' he said. 'An' you could get into a lot of trouble takin' black market meat.' But my grandmother did not refuse the gift and it certainly made catering for Christmas a lot easier.

Afterwards, I went home with my mother to sit the scholarship for Letchworth Grammar School, while my aunt and cousin returned to Eccles Road, leaving John and Ann at Necton.

In 1943 the ban on church bells was lifted for Easter Sunday. In May we heard about the dambusters' raid and in June we were told the signposts would be re-erected in rural areas. 'Now I do reckon I could find me rud to Swaffham,' my grandfather said, with heavy irony.

As well as looking after what she called her 'mums', Eliza was still sitting with the dying, making sure their last hours were as comfortable as possible and laying them out for the funeral. It must have been difficult when she had to look after her grandchildren as well, especially with Aunt Norah away in the Land Army, but by then Arthur had moved into Rest Cottage, which stood at the top of the Drift, opposite Hilda's parent's home, and she was able to send Ann up to play with Dulcie when she was called out on days when there was no school.

At school Ann had been using old envelopes to categorise items drawn on cards as part of her reading and arithmetic lessons, and she decided to teach three-year-old Dulcie the game. One day when the adults were out, they took all the tins and jars off the pantry shelf and removed their labels. Then Ann carefully cut out the pictures and placed them in envelopes, purloined from the stationery cupboard. The picture of a cow on a tin of milk went into an envelope labelled animals. Pictures of peas and beans went into the vegetable envelope. Similarly, illustrations depicting flowers and fruit were neatly cut out and placed in appropriate envelopes. As a school exercise it was probably excellent, but for the next few weeks, no one knew what they were likely to be given for their dinner.

Although I was living at home with my parents, it did not mean I had turned my back on Necton. I returned at the end of the summer term to spend the holiday with my brother and sister. The weather reflected the general feeling of optimism – it was a glorious summer. After a spring drought, rain came just at the right time for the crops and was followed by long spells of sunshine. We all went potato picking.

We were picked up in a lorry lined with forms, which reminded me of the tale of Necton's first bus, except that no one had taken the trouble clean it out. As soon as we arrived in the field we were allocated our positions. A tractor went down each row and turned over the crop, exposing the roots and it was the picker's job to extricate the potatoes and put them in a basket. You could either bend your back or kneel, both of which postures soon became very uncomfortable.

When your basket was full, you took it to a table where it was weighed and sorted; the inferior ones were thrown to one side to be fed to the animals, the rest were put in sacks for sale. In the middle of the day, we collapsed in the hedgerow to eat the sandwiches and lemonade we had brought with us. Getting up again to resume work was agony but no one was allowed to rest. When we got home that first night, we discovered Grandma had the copper on and the water was hot for a bath. With Epsom salts poured into it, it was bliss. The great consolation was that at the end of the week, there was a little pay-packet.

There was a lot of talk that winter and the following spring about the second front, which everyone confidently expected would bring an end to the war. The Germans apparently thought the invasion might be launched from the East Anglian coast and my grandmother's letters spoke of heavy raids. Mother would have liked to have gone to Necton to see for herself, but the Government put a ban on all travel within a ten mile width of the coast and though Necton was outside that area, travelling was a nightmare. It was obvious to everyone that something was about to happen and we waited expectantly.

Surrounded as it was by airfields, the inhabitants of Necton were used to planes going overhead at night, but one particular night stands out in my brother's memory. 'I was woken by a rumbling noise,' he said. 'I thought it was thunder at first, but it went on and on so I got out of bed to look out of the window. The sky was so black with aircraft you couldn't see the stars. I started to count them, but gave up long before they finished going over.' Grandma came up and tucked him in again and told him that it was nothing to worry about. 'They're ours,' she said. The next morning, the country learned that the Allies had landed in France, not only from the sea, but from the air. Thousands of airborne troops

had been put on to French soil by parachute and glider.

It was not all plain sailing. Men were still being killed and wounded, but advances were made and Paris was liberated in August. In September the blackout ended and Grandma thankfully took down the blackout curtains she had put up five years before, and John and Ann came home. On 8 May 1945, my 14th birthday, Germany surrendered. In July, at the end of the school term, we all went back to Necton.

After hearing all our news Grandma told us hers. There were new babies in the village and most of the evacuees had gone, though some liked Necton so much, they made their homes there. There had been deaths too, both as the result of the war, of illness and of old age. And she had heard from Alice.

Alice's son, John, was in England safe and well, for which she gave thanks. He had been part of the British Expeditionary Force sent to France at the beginning of the war and had been on his way to Paris when it surrendered. They had turned back to Dunkirk, from where he had been safely evacuated. He had been wounded in Sicily and spent eight weeks in hospital in North Africa before taking part in the Italian campaign and being slightly wounded again. Now he was back in England and expecting to be sent home very soon. He had married an English girl called Cecilia and had a small son, also called John, and Alice was over the moon about it. There was going to be a big family celebration when he got back.

We also learned that the pony had been put down and it had broken my poor grandfather's heart. It was getting on for 20 years old, past the age for useful work.

Mary and a friend standing beside the well with the pit in the background, c.1947.

When it could no longer pull the trap, it had been set free in the orchard, but it still needed to be fed and Grandad was a realist if nothing else. It had to go. 'It were old,' he said. 'We all hatta go in the end.' But the decision cast a shadow over us and no one wanted to go into the shed where the trap was kept.

Now there were no animals on the smallholding except a few chickens, a dog and two cats, one of which was reputed to be 19 years old. The red tape involved in keeping farm animals was too much for Grandad to cope with, but he was lost without them.

He was still talking about the seasons and farming, just as if he was still deeply involved, although he had been officially retired since 1937. He talked of the farming regulations and the newly introduced price guarantees that were supposed to last four years. 'It oon't be any different from the last time,' he said. 'I'm hully glad, I don't hev to worry about it no more. Things woon't ever be the same.' One of his biggest gripes was the cost of a pint of beer in the Good Woman, which he visited from time to time. Whisky, even supposing you could lay your hands on it, cost 25s a bottle, a week's wages to some people. Even my grandmother's 'brown milk' had shot up in price.

After staying a few days, Mother left us just as she had done in the years before the war and we were still in Necton when the first atomic bombs were dropped on Japan and the war in the Far East ended. There was a party in the village to celebrate and, leaving John and Ann with Grandad and Aunt Norah (in civvies again), my grandmother and I walked up the village to see what was happening. I remember her saying, 'I'll soon be 70, far too old for such high jinks.' 70, she said. I did not know it then, but she was still adding those four years to her age.

'Oh, you'll live to be 100,' I said airily.

'I hope not,' she said. 'I should hate to be a burden on my family and at that age, you don't have much choice.'

'You would never be a burden. You're as sprightly as Mum.'

'Things will change,' she said. 'Nothing stays the same. You'll see.''

It was an unusually serious conversation for her, but she soon brushed it aside and when we arrived in the village she was greeted enthusiastically by everyone. So many of the younger people had been brought into the world with her help; there were even second generations of her 'babies' and few of the older inhabitants had not been touched by her kindness. She said to me once, 'Do you know what you have to give away if you want to keep it?' And when I shook my head, she teased me, 'Think.' But I could not and she smiled. 'Love, Mary, love. Think on it.'

The End of an Era

AT FIRST, the change my grandmother had predicted was slow to arrive, simply because now the war was over, all everyone wanted to do was to get back to normal and do whatever they were doing when it started, but shortages and rationing continued. Over a year after the war ended bread and flour were rationed, two of the few items to escape during hostilities.

The new year of 1947 brought arctic conditions to the country; even the sea froze off the coast of Norfolk. There were 14ft snow drifts and the people of Black Drift had to dig themselves out. My grandparents would have been snug enough in their little cottage but there was a drastic shortage of coal caused by a series of unofficial strikes in the newly nationalised coal industry, and the railways, which had been running at full stretch throughout the war and were in need of drastic refurbishment, could not deliver what there was. The Prime Minister spoke to the nation on the radio and appealed for people to economise by wearing an extra jumper instead of turning up the heat and to use candles to save electricity, which had my grandparents laughing aloud. Electricity indeed. Chance would be a fine thing, they were still using heavy accumulators to power the wireless.

A sudden thaw in February brought floods. The fields of Necton were covered in sheets of water and the pit was full to the brim. No one could get on the land and spring planting was very late. The milk ration was reduced to half a pint a day, newspapers were cut back to the wartime four pages to save paper, holidays abroad were banned and petrol could only be had for essential purposes, giving rise to the phenomenon of the 'spiv' and a new kind of black market. 'Land fit for heroes, my eye!' my grandfather said contemptuously. He had seen it all before.

The potato crop was so poor that in November the unprecedented happened and potatoes were rationed. People were being told to eat more pasta and rice. 'Where have we heard that afore?' Grandma said, with a smile. But there was some cheerful news. Audrey had given birth to Sylvia, her second daughter.

In July 1948, the National Health Service came into being, with its promise to take care of the people from the cradle to the grave. Everything was free: false teeth, spectacles, hospital treatment and the services of the GP and midwife. My grandmother, who had in any case virtually retired, became well and truly redundant. But people could not get out of the habit of calling her in.

Arthur was wakened one night by someone throwing pebbles at his bedroom window and banging on the door. Old Mrs Walker, who lived down the lane next to Black Drift and had not been outside her garden gate in years, had struggled as far as my Uncle's and was intent on rousing him from his bed. 'Fetch your ma, Arthur,' she called, when he opened the window. 'Tell her my owd man 'as bin an' gone an' died.' So he pulled on his trousers and a shirt and went to fetch his mother. And of course, she went.

After that she attended no more confinements and sat with no more dying patients, nursed no one back to health, except those of her own family who needed her. But that did not mean she lost interest or would not give advice if she was asked for it. If she was out in the village and saw an expectant mother she knew, she would always ask how she was and wish her well.

Dr Townend, with whom Grandma had worked so closely, retired in 1949 and when she heard he was leaving the village, she organised a collection to give him a present. She kept the letter he wrote thanking her:

Dear Ma

Some few days ago there arrived from Norfolk for me, a very beautiful leather album containing several hundred signatures of my many friends and patients of my old practice.

I had heard rumours that a presentation was to be made but had hoped that I had 'scotched' this project and it had been abandoned.

I have done nothing whatever to deserve this and feel almost overwhelmed. I am, indeed, touched by the kindness of the thought and yet feel deeply honoured that my services seem to have been thought so highly of as to merit the magnificent present. My twenty-seven years in Norfolk were very happy ones and when the time came to leave, it was a great wrench but I felt the time was not far off when my best efforts would not

reach my rather rigid standard and I found my last few months as much as I could manage.

With the cheque, I am going to purchase something in silver which will serve to remind me always of the wonderful kindness shown to me by all you dear Norfolk folk.

With a lump in my throat I can only say 'thank you' but, knowing me as you all do, you will know my appreciation is very real.

Yours appreciatively

R O T Townend.

P.S. I have been ill – very suddenly – and had to be rushed into hospital and operated on. Would have liked you beside my bed the first night or so afterwards! You and I have sat at various bedsides for many a long hour together, helping new arrivals – and helping out the old ones. I hope Ong is well, not forgetting 'bag o' fleas.' ROT

'Bag o' fleas,' was the name given to me by the good doctor when he learned my name was VanderVlies.

Grandma and Grandad were both getting older now and moved more stiffly. My grandfather particularly seemed a bit breathless and forgetful and sometimes looked a little lost.

Eliza with granddaughter Mary.

Walter and Eliza outside the hut, 1948.

The shed Walter repaired with clay lumps, now used for storage. The black building behind it is the old stable, known as the 'end shud'. They are all that is left of the original buildings now.

But that doesn't mean he was inactive; he was out and about as much as ever, it was almost as if he felt guilty if he was in the house during daylight hours. When the wall of the cartshed fell down he rebuilt it using 'clay lumps' he had made with clay he dug from the pit. I wonder if my grandmother showed him how to do it or whether it was just one of the many country skills he had.

Although we saw each other less frequently in the ensuing years, we were, thanks to my grandmother, a close-knit family and Black Drift was a central point in all our lives. The grandchildren were growing up, the older ones going out to work, and leading their own lives, but everyone would now and again take a trip to Necton, though now travel was faster and easier, it was more likely to be a day trip.

The Yorkshire contingent also visited, but that was a longer journey and they usually stayed a few days. Alfred, who became the father of five when his daughter Valerie was born in May 1949, was still being teased about his itchy feet though he had lived in the same place for over 20 years. His urge to travel seemed to be satisfied by his job on the railways as a bill sticker. All the old propaganda posters of the war, things like, 'Is your journey really necessary' and 'Hitler will send no warning. Always carry your gas mask.' were being torn down and bright new ones, advertising holiday destinations, were being put in their place.

No visitor ever left Black Drift empty-handed. It might be half a dozen eggs, or a jar of home-made jam, a packet of tea or biscuits in a fancy tin. Sometimes it would be a brooch or an ornament, even half a dozen wine glasses. When the time came for you to leave, a small parcel was put into your hand or tucked into your bag. It gave my grandmother so much pleasure, none of us, however well off we were, would have dreamed of refusing.

When my husband and I became engaged in 1949, one of the first people I wanted to tell was my grandmother, so we cycled to Necton from Great Yarmouth where we now lived so that I could introduce him to her. While we were there, we went for a walk down the Drift. It had not changed, except, as is the way of things remembered from childhood, everything seemed smaller. 'Oh, there's change in the air, you can be sure,' my grandmother said when I mentioned this to her. 'We had the men from the electricity board down here the other day, the village is getting electricity and they talk about bringing the cables down the Drift.'

It was quite a way down from the top and they were told they would have to pay for that stretch themselves. The same thing happened when the Council came, talking about water mains and sewerage pipes. There was no way my grandparents could afford it, even sharing the cost with their neighbours across the Drift. 'We ha' managed without all these years,' Grandad said. 'We kin manage the rest on our lives, I reckon.'

I married in November 1949 and in January 1951, my son, David, was born, making Walter and Eliza great-grandparents for the first time. In the same month they became grandparents again. My Aunt Emma had a second son, Colin, 12 years after Ronald was born. My grandmother did not attend that birth, but she still had a contribution to make; Ronald was sent to stay with her until it was all over.

Grandad sold the field on the other side of the orchard for £100 and spent more of his time pottering close to the house. He always seemed to have plenty he wanted to do, if it was only digging the garden, mixing up the chicken food and scything the long grass in the orchard. But without the animals it was never enough and, unable to sit still or even stay indoors, he took to wandering round the village, looking over other people's fields, assessing how well they were doing and stopping to pass the time of day. Though no longer actively farming, he took a keen interest in what his neighbours were doing and was free with his advice, some of it not particularly welcome. 'Time you were gettin' on with drillin' that top field.' Or, 'That hay's a-gooin' to be ruined of you don't get it in, it'll rain come morning.' But because he was respected and liked, no one told him to mind his own business – at least not to his face.

Grandma was as active as ever. She was a founder member of the Necton Branch of the Women's Institute, which had been formed in 1952. Its forerunner had been an unofficial gathering they called 'the Toot'. The WI gave women a taste of organising their own affairs as well as confidence in airing their own opinions instead of repeating those of their husbands. There was a choir and a knitting circle, a drama group and debating forum, all of which my grandmother participated in, never missing a meeting until a year or so before she died.

She persuaded Grandad to join the Silver Thread Club with her and they would go together to the meetings, enjoying

Eliza and Walter on the occasion of their Golden Wedding in 1954, taken inside the cottage. The door behind them leads to the stairs. Photo courtesy of Eastern Counties Newspapers Ltd.

complete. And in the same year, my daughter, Sally, was born.

On 30 July 1954, beside a photograph of my grandparents standing outside the door of the cottage cutting a cake, the *Eastern Daily Press* reported that:

Mr and Mrs Ong of Black Drift Necton are celebrating their golden wedding quietly at home today. They were married at Necton Parish Church. Mr Ong, who is 83, was born at Necton. He started work at twelve earning 1s 6d a week, looking after sheep. When they were married his weekly wage was 10 shillings. They have seven children – two sons and five daughters, including twins. They have thirteen grandchildren and two great grandchildren. Because of heart trouble Mr Ong has to rest a great deal but his seventy-six-year old wife, Eliza, is very active. She still does her own housework, cooking and washing and also belongs to a number of village organisations. They are both members of the Necton Silver Thread Club.

whatever activity was on offer, sharing a gossip and having a cup of tea and a piece of cake.

In 1953, the year of the east coast floods, Audrey gave birth to Paul. Walter and Eliza's tally of 14 grandchildren was now

Almost a whole lifetime encapsulated in one short paragraph, although someone had miscounted the number of grandchildren and I am sure it was not my grandmother. She knew everyone's birthday and we all received cards on the appropriate day. She would amuse herself and us by counting how many there were in each month and she not only knew the day and the month, but the year. So how could she possibly not have known her own date of birth? I refuse to believe she did not, but the four years was still being added to her age.

Great-grandchildren, David and Sally, in the garden of the cottage, 1954.

My husband had joined the Territorials when he came out of the army and when he went on one of his annual camps I took David and Sally to stay for a few days at Necton, just as I had done as a child. I had to teach the children the intricacies of going to bed by the light of a candle, washing in a basin in the bedroom and going down the garden to the loo. I took them down the Drift for a walk, showed them the lay-down tree, the cart shed and the stable, still a storehouse of antiquities though there was no pony. They sat on the little Windsor chair, peered down the well

Walter bathing his great-grandson, David, in the back-place, 1954.

while I kept a tight hold on them, and were bathed in the old tin bath.

While we were there we went to a fête being held on the recreation ground. My grandmother was helping with the teas and cake stall and we helped her carry her con-

Fred Painter (at the microphone) introducing Norman Painting (alias Philip Archer of the BBC programme) who opened Necton fête in July 1953.

tribution, including the precious tea set. The children had a ride on the 'train', which was a small tractor pulling a number of wooden carriages round the field and had ice creams and buns. While we were there we had a stroll round the village. It was still recognisably Necton and the school looked just the same from the outside, but there were also many new houses. The fine oaks which had once surrounded Necton Hall had gone and so had most of the Hall.

'What happened to the Hall?' I asked my grandmother when I rejoined her.

'Mr Somerset de Chair sold it,' she said. 'It change hands two or three times, but no one lived in it. There was talk of turning it into flats and then of making it into a school, but it was riddled with dry rot and they pulled it down.'

'How sad,' I said.

She shrugged. 'Times change, things can't go on the same forever. '

'What happened about the electricity?' I asked, as she trimmed the lamp wick that evening and we sat in the glow of its light after the children had been put to bed in the big double bed with its brass knobs and thick feather mattress, just as I had done as a child.

'Oh, nothing. Seems we'll hatta move anyway.'

'Move?' I was astonished. It was unthinkable.

'Yes. We've been told this house is unfit for human habitation.' She sounded really

Necton Hall, just before it was demolished. Photo courtesy of Eastern Counties Newspapers Ltd.

down and I could understand it. It had been her home most of her married life and she loved it, but more than anything she was worried about how Grandad would cope with a move.

'Where will you go?'

She shrugged. 'We can't buy anything that's for sure, we'll just hatta wait and see what turns up.'

She told me that someone suggested they ought to qualify for supplementary benefit and she had decided she had nothing to lose by applying for it. 'They need Grandad's signature,' she said. 'But I dussn't tell him what it was for. He never would hev agree.'

'What did you do?'

'I told a little white lie.' She smiled. 'I say it was to get a rise in our pension. It weren't so far from the truth, was it?'

My husband came to fetch us the following day and I never visited the cottage in Black Drift again. The following year, my grandparents were allocated a small Council bungalow in St Andrew's Lane. Getting Grandad there was the problem. At first he refused to budge and a welfare officer came to try and persuade him. 'It will be lovely for you, Mr Ong. There's electricity and a bathroom and a proper toilet indoors. Hot water any time you want it. Surely you would rather have all modern conveniences than...' She looked round the little cottage and shrugged her shoulders deprecatingly, which annoyed Eliza and incensed Walter.

'I ha' lived here most on my life and I mean to die here,' he said. 'You kin't mek me go.'

'Mr Ong, I am afraid we can. This place is not fit to live in.'

I think my grandmother ushered the woman out before Grandad could explode. 'Leave it to me,' she told her. 'I'll persuade him.'

I don't know how she did. Another little white lie, I expect, something to the effect that if he did not agree, they would be separated and put into homes and that would mean Norah would be homeless too. And no doubt Aunt Norah added her arguments, which might have borne a little more weight with him.

On the day of the move Walter was coaxed up to the bungalow, but Eliza had to keep a close eye on him, in case he decided to wander back. They busied themselves about the new house and garden. Someone had sent a bouquet of yellow roses as a welcome to their new home and Norah, who certainly had 'green' fingers, took a cutting and planted it in the ground by the back door. Amazingly it struck and flourished. It was not the only thing Aunt Norah 'planted'; even the new shop-bought linen post sprouted.

The auction was held a few days later. Grandma daren't let Grandad out of her sight, knowing it would break his heart to see their possessions go under the hammer, nor could she bear to go herself. Everything was laid out in the orchard for anyone to come and 'gawp' at, as my grandmother put it. The horsehair sofa and its matching chairs, bedroom sets, beds, the big kitchen table, chamber pots, cupboards, tin baths, the mangle, the flat irons and the cobweb-

by contents of the stable were all laid out to the sky. None of it, so lovingly looked after for all the years they had lived there, made more than a few pounds, though nowadays they would be considered 'collectables' or antiques. The item that realised the most was the old hut, which had been their bedroom. It made £80.

At the end of the day, Black Drift as a home ceased to exist and not long afterwards, as if Fate was closing the book on it, the roof blew off in a gale and was replaced with corrugated iron by Mr George Tuffs, who had bought the land, and thereafter it was used as a store. It changed hands twice more and was eventually bought by Mr and Mrs Saunders who continued to live on the other side of the Drift until they built a new bungalow on the pasture behind the old cottage. The house across the Drift, once my mother's childhood home, is now occupied by their son and his family.

Walter was feeling his age now and there were odd signs of growing confusion, which my grandmother noted but did nothing about. He would go off into the village and forget where he was and friends and neighbours would gently guide him home. But he always knew when Thursday came round because that was the day Dulcie had a half day off from work and he would walk down to Rest Cottage, to sit for a while and have a cup of tea with her. Then he would say, 'I ha' had enough now, tek me home.' Dulcie would carefully steer him past the top of the Drift and along the lane to the new bungalow.

On one occasion, he wandered into the kitchen of a farm in Ivy Todd and without saying a word, sat in the chair beside the hearth and began taking off his boots to the

Eliza's sister Alice, with her daughter Edna (left) and English daughter-in-law Cecilia, at the end of World War II.

consternation of its occupants. Someone from the house went to fetch Arthur who came and said, 'Put your boots back on, Pa, you hatta come alonga me.' and he went like a lamb. Another time, he went up to the Tuns corner and tried hitching a lift to Dereham, saying he was going to market. Luckily he was known to the driver of the car who picked him up and was taken home. But as far as Walter was concerned it was not home and that was where he wanted to be.

'He get muddled,' Grandma told me. 'He's always getting up at the crack of dawn to go to work.'

'What work?' I asked.

She smiled. 'Only he knows that. The welfare want to put him in a home, but while I've got my health and can look after him, he's stopping here. I've got Norah to help me, I told them, so they let us alone.'

I was in the kitchen watching her mix cakes to bake in the Aga, which, I suppose, was not so different from the old range she was used to. When they came out of the oven they were as light as I remembered them. She put half a dozen in a box to take to the old lady who lived next door. 'She's a poor old thing,' she said. 'And all on her own.'

Norah laughed. 'She's a lot younger than you are and you know it.'

But it did not stop her going. Nor did she stop her village activities and she still kept her wonderful sense of humour.

In 1955, Alice died in Canada. It made Eliza very sad to think they had never been able to meet again, but she continued to correspond with Alice's daughter Edna, who kept her abreast of the news out there. Alice's eight children had between them given her 41 grandchildren and Eliza wished she could have met some of them.

She was to get her wish because a little later, Edna came to England on a visit with her husband and their two children. 'We were touched by such a close caring family,' Edna wrote to me. 'After a lovely meal, Aunt Eliza invited me into the kitchen for a 'private chat'. She closed the door and saw that I was comfortably seated, then she drew a stool up to the kitchen cupboard, climbed up and opened the top cupboard door, reached back into it and brought out a packet of Woodbines. "He hasn't driven me to drink yet, but I need this," she said. I think Uncle Walter had Alzheimer's, though at that time they did not have a name for it. She told me she would lock the bedroom door thinking he was napping and he would go out through the window and wander aimlessly about the neighbourhood, as if he were "going to work."'

With two small children, they had to leave early to go to the Good Woman where Grandma had booked them in for the night. After they had settled the children they went down to the lounge to find Eliza there. She had been sad to say goodbye to them so soon and Norah had persuaded her to go and have another hour or two with them. It is puzzling that in all their conversation over that day and subsequent letters, there was never any mention of Eliza's other two sisters and Edna never knew of their existence. She is not even sure if her mother knew of them.

1956 was marked by the death of Eliza's aunt, Sarah Crockley, at the age of 89. She had been a true friend and staunch ally through thick and thin and Eliza was saddened by her passing, but she was not mor-

Eliza with all her children on the day of Walter's funeral. Norah is holding her mother's chair. The others are, left to right: Alfred, Doris, Gladys, Audrey, Emma and Arthur.

bid about it. She had seen so many come and go and as she said, 'We all hatta go in the end.'

In spite of her best efforts, Walter's health deteriorated and he died in 1958 after a stroke. The whole family assembled for the funeral. For the first time in years, all seven children were together. Besides the immediate family, Walter's sister Florence was there, Hannah's son Sidney and his wife, Arthur Crockley and his wife

and daughter, Mrs Clements and Mr Milford, the grocer, and many, many more, all came to pay tribute a stalwart countryman who had remained true to his roots all his life.

Eliza did as she always had, she pulled herself together and got on with her life. She and Norah lived together in the bungalow; but far from shutting herself away, she continued to live as full a life as possible. She went to the Silver Thread

The newspaper article covering the Women's Institute's 21st birthday at which Eliza cut the cake.

Club and the Women's Institute meetings and actively participated in all they did. When the WI celebrated its 21st birthday with a buffet meal and sherry, Eliza, its oldest member, cut the cake with flash bulbs popping. The family clubbed together to buy her a television and she enjoyed watching comedy programmes and debates.

Her grandchildren were growing up and marrying now and her tally of great-grandchildren was increasing, but she still remembered all their birthdays and had a wonderful memory for other things as well. 'I've

WI celebrates 21st birthday

NECTON Women's Insitute held their 21st anniversary party in the village hall and the president, Mrs. I. V. Bengeyfield welcomed guests from Holme Hale, Fransham, The Pickenhams, Castleacre, Sporle, Foulden, Swaffham, Great Cressingham and Bradenham. About 70 people attended.

Special guests were Mrs. E. Sanderson, the VCO who was at the inaugural meeting Mrs. E. Makins the first president of the Institute and Mrs. B. Kemp a past president.

Sherry with a buffet meal was enjoyed. Mrs. W. Ong the oldest member aged 94 cut the birthday cake which was decorated in Institute colours.

Entertainment was provided by members of the Swaffham Players.

Mrs. Staines. A competition for a picture from autumn leaves was won by Mrs. Allsop, Mrs. Pritchard, Mrs. Giles, and Mrs. Hall. Birthday posies were made by Mrs. Bidewell.

Clenchwarton

Members of Clenchwarton WI were guests of Tilney St. Lawrence WI at their Christmas fair opened by Mrs High, of West Walton. Refreshments were served followed by a display of physical education and yoga.

Praise for bulb growers' co-operative

Warm praise for the South

Eliza (centre), Vi Fickling (left) and Ethel Palmer enjoy a joke at the Silver Thread Club Christmas party. Photo courtesy of the Lynn News and Advertiser.

Eliza with granddaughter Ann's son, Derek, 1960.

Eliza, aged 86, gets behind the wheel of her granddaughter Valerie's mini, 1968.

lived in six reigns,' she was very fond of saying and then proceeded to name them in the correct order. 'I've seen the bicycle and the motor car and the aeroplane come in. We didn't have electricity or the wireless when I was a girl, let alone television. Now we're off into space. I wonder where it will all end, though I shan't be here to see it.' She paused and then she went on. 'Still, we don't get mothers and babies dying like we used to and no one is starving. I could tell you some tales that'd make your hair curl.'

Her one worry, she told me, was what would happen to Norah when she died. 'Mr Right never came along, she'll be all alone,' she said. I assured her, as others in the family must have done, that Aunt Norah was perfectly capable of looking after herself and she was not wanting in friends and family.

Hilda became ill with cancer in the 1960s and Arthur, who was now working as a caretaker at a Swaffham school and cycled backwards and forwards each day, was himself unwell and continually breathless. He was sent to Papworth Hospital for a heart operation, which gave him a new lease of life, and Hilda seemed to be in remission, much to Eliza's relief.

In the spring of 1972, I was shocked when my mother rang me to tell me Norah had died. 'Aunt Norah?' I repeated, unable to believe it. 'What happened?' I assumed it must have been because of an accident. Norah had never had a day's illness in her life and had never visited a doctor.

'It was cancer of the throat. She told Mother she couldn't swallow and Mother persuaded her to go to the doctor. He sent her straight to hospital and they kept her in.'

'When did all this happen?'

'Last week. She died last night. Arthur's just rung me.'

'Oh, poor, poor Grandma.'

The only consolation was that Norah had not suffered long. 'To think I was worried about what she would do when I was gone,' Grandma told me later. 'I never dreamed she would go first.'

The following January, Alfred died of a heart attack aged 59. A deeply religious man, he had been churchwarden, grave-digger and sole bell-ringer, which he did using two arms and one leg, and was known in Yorkshire as 'the parson without a collar'. That same year Hilda lost her valiant fight against cancer. Grandma, mourning herself, comforted the grieving and coped stoically with her own life.

My daughter was married that year and we dearly wanted my grandmother to attend, but it was a long journey and she did not think she was up to it. We sent her Sally's bouquet, which she wrote and told me cheered her up no end.

On one of my later visits she told me she had had 'a bit of a fall'. She had decided to clean out the kitchen cupboards and as some of them went up to the ceiling, it meant climbing up on a chair and from there on to the draining board to reach them. 'I slipped,' she said, laughing. 'Down I went and end up sitting in the sink with me feet in the air and me bloomers showing.'

'How on earth did you get out?'

'It were a bit of a puzzle but I manage in the end. Don't you go telling Arthur now.'

I did not say anything to Arthur, but he must have found out because after that a home help visited the bungalow every morning to do the housework, although my grandmother continued to do her own cooking. She still went to her meetings in the village, someone would always pick her up in the car and take her. On one occasion she won the glamorous granny competition at Necton's annual horticultural show.

The night the Three Tuns closed for the last time, my grandmother said she would dearly like to have a last drink there. So, together with Arthur and my mother, who was staying a few days, she walked up to the pub and discovered half the village had the same idea. She sat in the corner of the crowded bar, sipping a glass of 'brown milk' and talking about the changes since she had worked there. When Charlie Passant, the landlord, called time everyone spilled out on to the car park, saying good night to each other, before wending their way homeward. Grandma was smiling. 'I thought you'd be sad,' my mother said.

'Why? I've got nothing to be sad about. Besides, I've got a souvenir.' She laughed and opened her handbag. Nestling inside was the glass she had been drinking from.

She was becoming quite frail physically but was mentally as alert as ever. By now everyone was talking about her reaching her 100th birthday but she maintained she did not want to be 100.

Eliza's diary for 1976 is full of the weather and her visitors. Besides her home help, a Mrs Sayer, various members of the family and her many friends visited her, making sure she had food in the house and coal in the box beside the fire and a cup of tea. Sometimes they brought a whole meal, ready to warm up and eat. She looked forward to them coming and it was a poor day when she wrote, 'Only the home help today.'

The spring was cold and wet and there was snow as late as April. Eliza had bouts of bronchitis, resulting in a few blank days in her diary. 'She foxed us many times,' I was told by Mrs Bengeyfield, one of my grandmother's great friends and, like her, a stalwart of the village community. 'She would be so ill and then recover and when we went to see her she would be sitting up looking like a duchess, which she was.'

Saturday 24 April, my mother's birthday, was the last entry for over a month. They resumed on 29 May, her own birthday, when she noted: 'I had 33 cards, lovely flowers and plants.' By June she was talking about the weather being warm and Arthur bringing her strawberries and ice cream. In July she wrote that she was dressed for the first time for three weeks and had heard that Doris was home from hospital where she had gone for an operation.

That summer was the hottest for 250 years; ponds and reservoirs became empty and everyone had to be careful of the water they used. The ground was so parched it crazed and cracks appeared in the walls of new buildings. Getting to sleep was a problem and my grandmother, always used to rising early, woke one morning and fancied a cup of tea. She got out of bed and slipped on the linoleum, putting her hand out to break her fall.

'I sat on the bed and looked at my arm,' she told me when I visited her later. 'And I thought, "I ha' been and gone and done it now."'

When the home help arrived some two hours later, she sent for an ambulance and my grandmother was taken to King's Lynn hospital. Her entry the next day, more spidery than usual, simply said: '10 days in hospital.'

On 3 August she was sent home with her arm in plaster. She wrote in her diary that night, 'Arthur here to get me to bed. Arm stiff. A lot of pain.' And next day, 'Nurse come in to see what can be done for me. Can't get on by myself.' And the following

day, 'Sent to hospital again.' A week later she was still in Swaffham hospital but, according to her diary, improving. On the 25 August she returned home.

By now her writing was very shaky and difficult to decipher. On the last day of August she wrote, 'Nurse come in and also Social worker to tell me about going into Westfield Home in Swaffham for one month.' That night there was a terrible thunderstorm and the weather broke.

On Monday 6 September, she was writing again, 'The organiser come about getting me into Westfield.' And the next day, 'Have been and looked at the home. Going on 13 September for a month to see if I like it. On the 13 September she wrote, 'Come into Westfield at 11.30. It will take time to get used to it all before I think about how I'll go on. Everything fresh to get on with but will try for the sake of the family.' On the 18th, in very shaky handwriting indeed, she wrote, 'Still in Westfield. Now to stop for good. Had five weeks here now.'

When I was reading it after she died, I thought that was her last entry, but flipping over the pages I found one for 1 January 1977. 'Started the new year with a big dinner, pheasant and white sauce. Drinks in the evening. ... (I can't decipher the name) was a bit tipsy and wished everyone Happy New Year, but not very happy for me.'

At the very end of the book, as a sort of postscript, she had written. 'Set out at 12.30. Had a big day with most of the family, as it was five generations. Met with the new baby.'

In March 1977, my own granddaughter had been born and when she was five weeks old we took her to Swaffham to see

my grandmother. She was sitting in a room with chairs all round in a circle and in every one of them was an old person in differing degrees of fragility and mental awareness. That was what she had meant by 'set out'. She had had her hair done and was bright as a button, but very frail. Against that background, Eliza made the acquaintance of her great-great-granddaughter, Nicola. She wanted to nurse her.

'I won't drop her,' she said, sensing Sally's reluctance. 'I've looked after hundreds of babies and I haven't dropped one yet.' Nicola was duly handed over and my grandmother drew off her wedding ring and slipped it over Nicola's thumb. 'There, I want you to have that,' she said. 'I shan't need it any more.'

I had a terrible job choking back the tears, but my grandmother was cheerful and so I was determined not to let her down by blubbing. Later a photographer from the *Eastern Daily Press* came and took pictures, one of which appeared in the newspaper with the caption 'Five generations.'

As we left, I said to her, 'The next celebration will be your hundredth birthday and you'll get a telegram from the Queen.' fully believing, as everyone else did, it would be the following May. I received the usual reply, 'I don't want to be a 100. I don't want a telegram.'

She was very ill with bronchitis in January 1978. My mother and Arthur were both with her on the evening of the 19th, although it was snowing hard. Grandma was quite lucid and worried that the weather would stop them getting home.

'Do you go,' she said, as always more concerned for them than for herself. 'I'm going to have a sleep now and when I wake up I shall have a nice cup of tea.' She paused a moment, then said. 'Look the sun is shining. You'll be all right now.' Outside the night was black as pitch and cold as charity; there was certainly no sun. Mother thought she had mistaken the electric light above the bed for the sun, but I wonder – did she see sunshine in a place no one else could see?

Mother kissed her goodbye and left to catch her bus. Arthur stayed a little longer, but when she appeared to be sleeping peacefully, he too left. A neighbour had given him a lift and was waiting to take him home. He had hardly got in the door when he received a telephone message to return to Swaffham. In spite of the worsening weather, they made it back. But he was too late. She had died in that last sleep.

My mother, too, received a call and tried to go back, but because of the snow she was able to go no further than my sister's at Norwich. Ann and her husband took her to Swaffham the next morning.

The church was packed to the doors for her funeral. Sitting at the front with the family, I could only see them through a blur of tears when I looked back. I remember wondering how many of that large congregation had been brought into the world by my grandmother. Afterwards we went to Arthur's bungalow and I renewed my acquaintance with Philip and others of my cousins I had not seen since the war. We tried not to be sad, because she would not have wanted us to be and talking about her

Five generations. Eliza holding her great-great-granddaughter, Nicola, with Mary, Doris and Sally looking on, 1977. Photo courtesy of Eastern Counties Newspapers Ltd.

and conjuring up little incidents in the past, we realised that most of our memories were happy ones.

It was Arthur, her executor, who found the letter among the mass of documents, photographs and newspaper cuttings she kept. It was on a tiny sheet of paper in an envelope no bigger than a postcard and addressed: 'To the Family, All of You, Hope everything will be as I wish.'

The letter was dated 4 July 1958, soon after my grandfather's death. In it she had written, 'I wish Norah to take over the home and furniture for her own use. What she don't want to keep she can sell, do what she think best. I would like her to keep my watch in the family. Hope this will be a help to all the family and help each other. Your loving Mother.'

There was a PS, written a year later, 'Rachel have got my watch as she wished for it. I would like Arthur to have my sitting room clock.'

After Norah died so unexpectedly, she had made a proper will, drawn up by a solicitor, dividing everything equally between her surviving children, but the tiny letter lay forgotten among her treasures.

The funeral was extensively reported under the headline 'Mother of Necton dies at 99.' It went on, 'Mrs Eliza Ong, former district nurse and midwife who was known locally as 'The Mother of Necton' has died in her hundredth year. She was probably the village's oldest inhabitant and failed by only three months to become a centenarian and so receive a special telegram from the Queen, something she and her family hoped she would achieve.' It went on with a potted history of her life and a list of the mourners, including all the

'Mother of Necton' dies at 99

Mrs E. Ong

Mrs Elizabeth Ong, a former district nurse and midwife who was known locally as "The Mother of Necton", has died in her hundredth year.

She was probably the village's oldest inhabitant, and failed by only three months to become a centenarian and so receive a special telegram from the Queen, something she and her family hoped she would achieve.

Mrs Ong had been a midwife and district nurse from 1920 to 1948, and used to cycle to all her cases.

The book of confinements she attended show that her payments were what families could afford — there are a lot of half-crowns listed. It was in 1926 that she was in Swaffham attenting a birth during an earth tremor.

Family

Mrs Ong's late husband was Mr Walter Ong, a smallholder who farmed at Cley Pit Farm. They had a family of seven, five of whom survive, and there are 14 grandchildren, 35 great grandchildren and one great-great grandchild.

She was a staunch member of the Women's In-

the Silver Threads Club. To the last she was a keen reader of the local news and matters relating to the village.

Mrs Ong, late of 31 St Andrew's Lane, Necton, had been a resident of Westfields Home for the Elderly at Swaffham for about 15 months, and it was there that she died.

The funeral service, at Necton Parish Church, was conducted by the Rev Peter Taylor. Mrs Jill Dobbs was organist.

Family mourners: Mrs D. Vandervlies, Mrs Dent, Mr A. Ong, Mr and Mrs R. Barnes, Mr and Mrs A. D. Took, Mr and Mrs B. Nichols, Mr P. Ong, Mr W. Ong, Mrs J. Long, Mr and Mrs Ronald Barnes, Mr and Mrs T. Kenning, Mr and Mrs Roy Barnes, Mr and Mrs R. Pickering, Mr and Mrs C. Barnes, Mr and Mrs P. Took, Mr and Mrs J. Vandervlies, Mr and Mrs A. Crockley, Mrs J. Spalding (Fakenham).

Mrs Bellamy was unable to attend.

Also at the service were Mrs I. Bengeyfield (rep the family and the parish council), Mrs West (rep matron and staff of the Westfield Home), Mrs R. H. King, Mrs W. Sayer, Mrs A. E. Whelan (rep Silver Threads Club), Mrs Whisker, Mrs Pimm, Mrs B. Diment, Mrs Hunt (rep Women's Institute), Mrs F. Pointer (also rep Mr Pointer), Mr R. H. King, Mrs E. Symonds, Mr and Mrs C. Chapman, Mrs E. Rogers (Swaffham), Mrs T. Tripp, Mr and Mrs E. Milson, Mr and Mrs C. C. English, Mr and Mrs J. Arbon.

Eliza's obituary. It did not get the facts right and would probably have made her smile.

representatives of the local organisations to which she belonged. Goodness knows what she would have made of it all. I can just imagine a wry smile. She had got her wish; she had not reached that magic number and looking back now, I am glad she did not. It would have been dreadful for her if the deception her grandmother had perpetrated all those years before, and which she had been so careful to maintain throughout her life, had been exposed.

A little later I had a letter from Mr and Mrs Makins' daughter-in-law, one of the many tributes paid to Grandma, who wrote:

I remember Mrs Ong in her younger days, bicycling about the village. She was nurse and comforter to so many and I always thought how sweet she looked with those lovely blue eyes. She never spoke of her early life, though of course she loved Black Drift. I remember riding down there and seeing her with the animals and your grandfather with his horse and cart – he loved the horses. We were all so fond of Mrs Ong... it is a great shame that these old people die without telling a lot of happenings, or if they do, people don't write them down and then they are lost...

I am glad I have been able, in some short measure, to redress that and put on record the story of someone who was a product of her time, but who was also remarkable for her compassion and insight and the great love she gave, not only to us her family, but to everyone around her.

Index